MW01134987

The Complete Guide to Miniature Australian Shepherds

Kearsten Williams

LP Media Inc. Publishing

Text copyright © 2019 by LP Media Inc.

www.lpmedia.org

Publication Data

Kearsten Willams

The Complete Guide to Miniature Australian Shepherds ---- First edition.

Summary: "Successfully raising a Miniature Australian Shepherd dog from puppy to old age" --- Provided by publisher.

ISBN: 978-1-70885-2-993

Editor - Dylan Tatum

[1. Miniature Australian Shepherds --- Non-Fiction] I. Title.

This book has been written with the published intent to provide accurate and authoritative information in regard to the subject matter included. While every reasonable precaution has been taken in preparation of this book the author and publisher expressly disclaim responsibility for any errors, omissions, or adverse effects arising from the use or application of the information contained inside. The techniques and suggestions are to be used at the reader's discretion and are not to be considered a substitute for professional veterinary care. If you suspect a medical problem with your dog, consult your veterinarian.

Design by Sorin Rădulescu

First paperback edition, 2019

Cover Photo Courtesy of Lindsey Condra - Stillwater Ranch Kennel

TABLE OF CONTENTS

CHAPTER 1
Miniature Australian Shepherd Facts

"When you own a Mini Aussie, you always have a best friend who is willing to stay by your side for life."

Ashley Bryan
Ashley's Aussies

What Is a Miniature Australian Shepherd?

Photo Courtesy of Mark A Delgado

The Miniature Australian Shepherd is, as the name suggests, a smaller version of the Australian Shepherd. Known by many as the Mini Aussie, it is sought after because of its beautiful coat, high level of trainability, and friendly nature. Mini Aussies are playful bundles of energy and make loving companions for active homes.

Mini Aussies should not be confused with either the larger Australian Shepherd, or the smaller Toy Australian Shepherd, which are both also registered with the American Stock Dog Registry (ASDR), the largest registry for Mini Aussie registered dogs. The Mini Aussie is able to perform many tasks that a larger dog can do, but are travel sized. They were initially bred as ranch dogs to herd livestock, and today they excel in many additional events, including: agility, herding trials, jumping to catch flying Frisbees, trick events and in entertainment.

History of the Miniature Australian Shepherd

To understand the history of the Miniature Australian Shepherd, you have to first understand the history of the Standard Australian Shepherd. Despite its name, the Australian Shepherd's origins hail from Europe and the breed was actually developed in North America.

While exact foundations are a bit of a mystery, it is generally agreed that the European Berger des Pyrenees, or Pyrenean Shepherd, breed arrived in the 1800s to North America. They accompanied traveling Basque Sheepherders, and were an important early influence. When the ranchers in North America saw the aptitudes of the breed, they began using them as herding dogs for livestock and adapting them to their own environments.

ADDITIONAL FACT

The U.S. Australian Shepherds Association (australianshepherds.org) does not recognize the miniature variety of Aussie Shepherd. The Miniature Australian Shepherd cannot be registered with the American Kennel Club (AKC) either. However, there is a Miniature Australian Shepherd Club of America (MASCA). Visit their website, mascaonline.com, for extensive information pertinent to this breed. It is "the oldest and largest extant parent club for the Australian Shepherd of the miniature variety." MASCA encouragvs quality breeding of Purebred Australian Shepherds of the miniature variety. The club discourages the sale of puppies to pet stores while encouraging responsible breeding through education. MASCA authorizes herding and obedience trials and competitions while also observing and promoting the ideal of the breed.

Many people are under the misconception that the Miniature Australian Shepherd is a mixed breed, but Miniature Aussies were never openly crossbred in order to reduce their size. Reputable breeders instead used selective breeding to set type, and as early as the 1960s, smaller Australian Shepherds were seen performing in rodeos.

A Californian Australian Shepherd enthusiast, named Doris Cordova, who noticed the smaller-sized dogs became obsessed with them. She gathered as many as she could, hoping to preserve the trait, and worked with a licensed veterinarian to create a breeding program. These dogs became an important part of the Miniature Aussies that we love today.

Some of the most well-known early dogs are registered with the National Stock Dog Registry (NSDR), the first organization to recognize Miniature Australian Shepherds. Cordova Spike was the first dog that association registered as a Mini. Crosswhite's Miss Kitty Fox, earned distinction as the first Miniature Australian Shepherd to receive a championship title in a show ring.

Physical Appearance

"There are three size classifications of Australian Shepherds (standard, miniature, and toy), along with 16 different coat colors. Most Aussies are also born with tails, but the breed standard is for docked tails."

Cayla Cox
CC Miniature and Toy Australian Shepherds

The Miniature Australian Shepherd breed standard, per ASDR rules, outlines:

A strong-featured, clean-lined head that is proportionate in the muzzle and skull length.

It has a sturdy front end and a deep chest.

Photo Courtesy of
Elizabeth Kidney

The dog's oval feet and its legs are proportionate to his body. The legs should be naturally pointed straight, not toed in or out, with a defining point between the stifle and hock. Ideal angulation in the shoulder is 45 degrees, with the hind end being similar for the purpose of balancing the dog when it is moving.

The body is slightly longer than he is tall, with moderate bone. The angulation in both the front and rear quarters should be the same, which contributes to the soundness of the dog's structure. This conformation helps the breed to maintain its agility.

The eyes of the dog should be almond shaped, not sunken in or protruding out-

10

Photo Courtesy of
Amanda Akagi

ward, with good fill in their face. They can come in several colors, including brown and blue.

The ears of the Mini Aussie should be set well on the head with them folding forward in "button" form, or to the side as "rose ears". Prick eared or hound eared is considered a fault in this breed.

One of the main identifiers of the Miniature Australian Shepherd is its gorgeous double coat. The breed's coat may be straight or wavy in texture with two different layers to the coat, and is described in the breed standard as a moderate texture. Underneath the outermost harsher guard-hair layer--which protects the dog from the elements-- is a softer undercoat. The undercoat serves to insulate from heat and cold. It needs to be well maintained with grooming, or matting can occur. Mini Aussies usually feature "feathering", flowing fringes of hair, around their front forelegs and their back hocks, as well as longer hair on their chest area and on the back of their hindquarters.

The Miniature Australian Shepherd's height is 14-18 inches from the ground to the top of its withers according to ASDR breed standards for both males and females. Miniature Australian Shepherds have a weight range of about 17 to 40 pounds depending on their diet and activity level, although there are no official weight restrictions outlined for the breed. Any weight is allowed.

Colors

Miniature Australian Shepherd coats come in a wide array of colors, but red and black are the foundation for the four accepted base colors: red, black and red and blue merle.

The merle pattern is a hallmark of the breed, and are simply the two base colors being affected by a modifying merle gene that causes spotted mottling in sometimes very striking patterns. Red merle modifies the red coat, creating lighter red patches, and blue merle modifies the black coat, creating blue-looking patches.

In addition, a Mini Aussie can have tan or white trim colors. With tan, also called copper, as well as white, the majority of the dog's coat will be the base color (or base color modified by merling). Tan and white markings can be on the head, legs, belly, and/or under the tail. Both tan and white can be as minimal as just a few hairs or very bold.

A tri is a dog with a base color and both white and tan markings.

A bi is a dog with a base color and one other color marking.

A self-colored dog has only base color, no white or tan markings.

Double merles

While science is still unraveling the merle pattern, right now the prevailing thought is that a single copy of the gene produces a beautifully colored dog, but two copies of the gene, commonly called "double merles", or homozygous merles, carry with them the enhanced risk of being deaf and/or blind.

Sometimes, double merles can be identified by an excess of white in non-standard areas of the body. But, this is not a firm rule. Many times, extra white can be caused by other genes, that have no health impacts to the dog.

Breed Behavior & Disposition

"Miniature Australian Shepherds are one of the most loyal breeds you will find. They bond extremely well to their human and make great companion animals. The intelligence of this breed is phenomenal, making them a great choice when choosing a breed."

Robert Kidd
Kidd's Toy Aussies

Miniature Australian Shepherds are very affectionate companions to their owners and families. They feel right at home curled up beside their owner.

Lively and playful, Miniature Australian Shepherds will keep up with active children all day, as well as are ideal running and hiking companions for athletic homes. But, if this workaholic breed does not have something to keep them occupied, they will find an activity to use up all that energy, which may include destructive habits like digging and chewing.

They are smart, busy, and highly intelligent and do require substantial amounts of training and boundary setting from their owners. When they get bored or if they are not trained, that's when they get into trouble!

*Photo Courtesy of
Lindsey Condra
Stillwater Ranch Kennel*

Some people are concerned about this breed nipping children. Mini Aussies, like any herding breed, does have a tendency to chase, because of the job they were bred to do instinctively, rounding up and directing live-stock on farms. Many still perform that function today.

As with any trait, there are levels of drives. So, with a proper match and good training, unwanted behavior should be manageable.

With this in mind, owners of any herding breed should plan to be dedicated to training their dog in acceptable behavior, and to correct as needed.

Miniature Aussies can be very protective of their owners. The breed standard, according to ASDR, clearly states that they are generally "stand-offish to strangers".

This points back to their historic use on ranches, where safety and security of the herd and family were of utmost importance.

Herding dogs by nature, Mini Aussies will herd cattle, goats, sheep and poultry. When these animals make sudden moves or run, they instinctive-ly chase after them. Miniature Aussies have even been known to jump up and run over the backs of a packed herd of these animals, in lieu of going around them, if it's the fastest way to cut them off and send a stray one back to the herd!

Is a Miniature Australian Shepherd Right for You?

Having a new dog or puppy should be a happy occasion. Before you purchase or adopt a Miniature Australian Shepherd, make sure you are able to accommodate the breed and that it is a good fit for you. Mini Aussies have become extremely popular, but they aren't for everyone.

There are pros and cons to having a Miniature Australian Shepherd. They are obedient companions with a tendency to want to please their own-er, and are extremely intelligent. You will be able to train your dog to per-form all sorts of tricks, but you may find that a quick-witted Mini Aussie might use something you have taught it against you!

The Mini Aussie is a wonderful choice if you have a family. Because of its energy level, the dog can easily keep up with children. It will be very loving and careful with your children. A Miniature Australian Shepherd will also be loyal to and protective of you and your child, regardless of its small stature. But you have to be sure to train your dog acceptable behavior around the family.

While the Mini Aussie's energy level can make it a wonderful choice for families with children and individuals with an active lifestyle, it can be risky for those who are more sedentary. If you work long hours and relax by curling up on the couch, you may not want to deal with your dog becoming bored and destroying your home, annoying your neighbors, escaping your yard, and starting other unwanted behaviors.

It is also important to recognize that it can be time-intensive to care for your Mini Aussie's double coat. You will need to buy the appropriate tools to maintain it, and if you neglect to groom your dog frequently, its fur will become matted and seasonal shedding more difficult. You must also check the dog's feathering for grass, leaves, stray twigs, and feces.

FUN FACT

Is a Mini Aussie Shepherd a good fit for you?

Are you active, an "outdoors type," persistent, patient, and do you have time for training a new four-legged family member? You might be just the right owner for a Miniature Australian Shepherd. The Mini Aussie is highly trainable, intelligent, vigorous, and a faithful companion. The Mini Aussie has a lifespan of approximately 13 years and grows to be 20-30 pounds. Smaller in stature than its fellow standard- sized Aussie, only 14-18 inches at the withers, it has many of the same qualities of the larger version of the breed.

Before obtaining a Mini Aussie, you should ask yourself these questions:

- Can I handle a high energy, busy dog?
- Do I have the time for a dog that must be exercised regularly?
- Do I have time to train a dog?
- Am I okay with having to groom a long-haired, double-coated breed?
- Do I want a dog that will live inside or outside?
- Do I need a smaller breed?
- Do I want a protective dog?
- Am I willing to make an 11- to 15-year commitment to raising a dog?
- Am I willing to train a dog that is intelligent and will get bored and destructive if not given proper care?

CHAPTER 2
Choosing a Miniature Australian Shepherd

"In my opinion, Australian Shepherds are one of the most loyal bred of dogs there are. They love their people and always want to please them. Their unique coloring and markings set them apart from the rest."

Gail Claborn
Circle 5 Aussies

Buying vs. Adopting

There are upsides and downsides both to buying a Miniature Australian Shepherd from a breeder and to adopting one from a shelter or rescue. Buying a dog can be a good option if you want a dog of show quality or to raise one from a puppy. Getting a dog from a shelter or adopting one from a rescue is a great way to help out a dog that is in need of a loving family.

Photo Courtesy of
Lindsey Condra
Stillwater Ranch Kennel

Buying a dog can be more expensive than adopting one, but you also typically know more information about the dog's background.

One of the biggest pros for buying a dog from a reputable breeder is genetic stability. The breeder will be able to tell you about the lines behind that dog. They should know if there are any health issues to be aware of in a puppy's history, or anything else of genetic concern. Responsible breeders also do extensive health testing to screen for the healthiest match of parents, which includes genetic disease panels, eye exams by licensed canine ophthalmologists joint x-rays, which are examined by a panel of veterinary specialists.

Adopting a dog can be slightly cheaper. If you choose to adopt, you may be able to find a Miniature Australian Shepherd for as low as $40 at a local shelter. If you visit a breed rescue, you could still be looking at upward of $200. While these dogs might be registered, dogs from reputable breeders do not usually end up in rescues. Breeders commonly have clauses in their sale contracts stating that they will take back dogs for owners who can no longer care for their dog.

HELPFUL TIP

Use Your Head and Heart When Choosing a Puppy

Do your research before purchasing your new pet. Observe both parents of the puppies, when possible, to check for behavior, temperament, and health issues. The Miniature Australian Shepherd comes in many different coat colors. Red merle, red tricolor, black tricolor, and blue merle are accepted and recognized coat colors in the Mini Aussie. It is not uncommon for the dogs to have two differently-colored eyes. The all-white Mini Aussie may be genetically predisposed to blindness, however. This anomaly can occur when two merle-colored Mini Aussies are bred. The breed may also experience hip dysplasia, certain eye disorders, epilepsy, and sensitivity to some medications. Being an educated consumer is an important first step when choosing a puppy.

However, it is important to realize that the decision whether to buy or to adopt goes beyond finances. While buying may ensure that your dog is closer to breed standards, some breeders fail to maintain humane conditions and breed dogs on a purely for-profit basis and do not care about the breed, breed standard, or quality of their dogs. If you go the buying route, be sure to choose a reputable breeder who is friendly, knowledgeable, and truly cares for their animals.

By the same token, adopting or rescuing a dog could give a Miniature Aussie who has been neglected or abused a renewed lease on life. Many

people are excited by the prospect of bringing home a cute new puppy, so older dogs often struggle to find homes. In some shelters, a dog that is unable to find a home may be put down. But also be aware that when you get a dog from a rescue, they generally have an unknown history, both behavioral history and genetic history. You need to be fully committed to the dog and handling any behavioral or health issues that arise after you adopt it.

When deciding whether to buy or adopt, finances can be an obvious hurdle, but you should also ask yourself what is most important to you in a canine companion and whether or not you have the time and energy to train a dog from puppyhood. Getting the dog is the cheapest part of pet ownership.

Tips for Adopting a Mini Australian Shepherd

Adopting a Miniature Australian Shepherd can be very different from buying a puppy from a breeder. When you adopt a dog, it could be mixed with another breed rather than being purebred. Given the popularity of Mini Aussies, it's unlikely that you will find a puppy in a shelter or for adoption. Be prepared to choose from adults.

- The Mini Aussie Rescue and Support Inc. (MARS) specializes in finding the right caregivers for homeless Miniature Aussies. There is a long application process to ensure that the dogs are placed with owners who will give them the love and attention they need. For more information, visit https://www.miniaussierescue.org/.

- Visit a local shelter. Although it is rare to find a Mini Aussie in a shelter, there is a possibility that your perfect pup is waiting for a home somewhere nearby.

- Check online, in newspapers, or other classifieds to see if there are any owners that are re-homing their pets due to moving or being unable to care for them anymore.

- Google Miniature Aussie rescues in your state or in surrounding states.

- Check with local pet stores such as PetSmart or Petco and visit them on adoption days.

- Contact your local veterinary clinics, as they may be able to help you locate a dog.

- When adopting a dog from a shelter, be aware of the dog's history if any was provided. Sometimes it is hard to know what a dog's background is, but knowing if it is kid-friendly or if it will get along with your other pets is an important factor in whether or not it is a good fit for you and your family.

- Make sure that the dog has no underlying health problems. If the dog does have problems, you will need to be prepared to deal with them at your own expense.

Photo Courtesy of Connie Watson Texas Miniature Aussies

Registered vs. Non-Papered

"Choose a breeder or rescue that is willing to answer all of your questions, and is willing to produce all of the parent's health testing information and the health records for the puppies to date. A good breeder will always want to stay involved and continue to be a resource as the puppy grows up."

Ashley Bryan
Ashley's Aussies

When purchasing a Miniature Australian Shepherd, you should have a clear purpose in mind. If you want a dog that can attend dog shows, are planning on breeding your dog to association standards, want to do any kind of registry-approved competition with your dog--such as agility, rally, or flyball--or want to know the lineage of your puppy; then buying a puppy with registration papers is important. Dogs with registration papers will often come with guarantees and there are some events that only registered dogs can attend. Be aware that purchasing a puppy with registration papers may be more costly than buying a dog without them.

Most Miniature Aussies are registered with American Stock Dog Registry (ASDR), Miniature Australian Shepherd Club of America (MASCA), or National Stock Dog Registry (NSDR). In the American Kennel Club (AKC), the Miniature Australian Shepherd is called the Miniature American Shepherd.

Photo Courtesy of
Mande Tharpe

Founded in 1956, NSDR was the first club in the United States to recognize the Mini Aussie as a breed.

ASDR and MASCA both offer competition opportunities for Mini Aussies today, including conformation, agility and herding.

If you only want a dog as a companion, having registration papers on your new Miniature Australian can still be beneficial to prove ownership of the dog or breed, as when traveling or renting.

Locating a Reputable Breeder

"Don't ever choose a puppy from a picture. Go meet the breeder and see where the puppies are being raised."

Cindy Harris
Rocky Top Kennels

It is important to be selective when searching for a Miniature Australian Shepherd breeder. One way to find a reputable breeder is to consult with acquaintances who have purchased Mini Aussies in the past and ask them if they recommend a breeder. They will be able to refer you to someone with whom they have had a positive experience, or steer you away from untrustworthy sources.

Breed registries often have breeder listings on their websites. These are also great starting places to begin researching breeders in your region.

Photo Courtesy of
Linda Overbay

A word of caution if you buy a puppy online sight unseen: When entering into an agreement with any breeder, be diligent in your research and understand the seller's reputation, either by speaking with others who have worked with them in the past or by consulting other trusted sources.

Never be afraid to ask your breeder questions about the pup you are going to buy, including asking for photos of the puppy if you are unable to see it in person.

Keep in mind, just because a breeder does not allow you to go to their house or kennel to meet the puppy does not mean that they aren't reputable. For their own safety, the puppies' safety and other dogs' safety, such as biosecurity risks; quite a few breeders no longer allow in-person visits. But they should be very open and willing to answer questions!

Breeder Contracts & Guarantees

"I would advise you to make sure that 1) parents have been health tested and are cleared from genetic diseases, 2) you are allowed to see the parents of the puppy and that they are not both merles as this can cause blindness and deafness in the merle puppies, and 3) the breeder offers a health guarantee on their puppies to allow your vet to evaluate the health."

Cayla Cox
CC Miniature and Toy Australian Shepherds

When you purchase a registered puppy, a lot, but not all, of reputable breeders will have you sign a contract. The contract usually includes your bill of sale and an application to the association with which the puppy is registered.

Applications for registration should include your puppy's date of birth, the sire and dam of your puppy, your puppy's coloration, the sex of your puppy, and other information about their identifying attributes.

If your goal is to breed your puppy when he or she is older, make sure you read the contract thoroughly! Many responsible breeders include stipulations that a puppy purchased from them cannot be bred. Responsible breeders understand that not everyone is willing to do the work and educa-

Photo Courtesy of Susan Hawkins

tion to breed healthy, structurally sound dogs. Limited registration, or "pet only", is to help maintain the breed standard.

Once terms are set, the breeder will usually give you a signed copy of the contract. Registration papers for the puppy can either be given to you, or the breeder will submit them to the appropriate registry to ensure that they are filed correctly. Be aware that there will usually be a fee from the registry to register your puppy.

Health Certificates

A puppy that is labeled "health certified" by the breeder will be up to date on its current vaccinations. This means the puppy has been cleared by the breeder's veterinarian and is considered healthy. Some health guarantees contain a clause that protects against your puppy dying. Health guarantees from breeders vary widely from breeder to breeder. These guarantees do not typically cover deaths caused by negligence or neglect, such as failure to properly care for the dog or the dog being hit by a vehicle or failure to vaccinate your puppy.

DNA Testing

A breeder may have a DNA test done on a litter of pups, and include results in their puppy packets for the new owners. DNA testing is very common practice and not overly expensive to do for a panel of diseases found in the Mini Aussie breed. The most common DNA testing is genetic testing, and is usually done with a simple swab of the puppy's cheek. This is done to avoid producing puppies with genetic diseases in the future.

Another non-disease reason for DNA testing a puppy is to prove parentage.

OFA Eye Exams

The Orthopedic Foundation for Animals (OFA) offers eye testing that is in conjunction with the Companion Animal Eye Registry (CAER). A licensed veterinary ophthalmologist performs a series of tests on puppies at about 16 weeks of age or older. These tests last anywhere from 30-40 minutes and can tell if a puppy has any vision loss or if it is a likely candidate to lose some or all of its sight in the future. This is also commonly done on dogs that are a part of a breeding program.

OFA orthopedic exams

OFA also maintains an official database and panels of veterinary specialists to evaluate hips, elbows and other joint x-rays that are submitted.

It's considered good form to have prospective parent dogs have passing scores before being considered as breeding prospects.

Having a pedigree full of healthy hips, for instance, won't guarantee your new puppy won't get hip dysplasia someday. But it does give him or her the best shot.

Selecting the Right Puppy

"If going to a rescue, try fostering the dog for a week before committing and have a veterinarian do a health exam. It is important to make sure an older dog will be a good fit for your family."

Ginny DeLeon
Broken D Bar Ranch

When selecting a puppy, it is important to find one whose personality fits your lifestyle. Mini Aussies have multiple levels of energy and drive, also called herding instinct. If you live a fast-paced lifestyle and spend a lot of time outdoors, then an active puppy will fit in quite nicely. However, if you live a sedentary life, or have small children, you may want to opt for a dog that is a bit less excitable. If you're particularly social and often entertain guests, be cautious of choosing a shy puppy that may have a hard time adjusting to an influx of new people and may be aggressive toward strangers as it grows up. Also be aware of the breed standard and understand that a dog in this breed accepting strangers has a huge training component in addition to a genetic and personality component.

It is important that you see these puppies in their natural state before you make your choice, unless you let your breeder select your puppy for you based on the personality and energy needs you have discussed with them at length. You should choose a day that works for both you and your breeder and spend time observing and socializing with the litter. Remember that not all breeders allow visitors to the litter for health and security reasons. If this is the case, ask your breeder about a phone call or video chat with the litter. Doing so will help you to see the unique components of each puppy's personality. Breeders who are committed to finding good homes for their puppies will not have a problem with you going the extra mile, but always be respectful of their time.

CHAPTER 3
Preparing Your Home for a Mini Australian Shepherd

"Have a safe, secure fenced yard and a warm place to sleep (preferably next to your bed). I, as a breeder always furnish, the toy they play with, a good harness and leash, a small bag of their puppy food and treats and a few puppy pads. Keeping them comfortable with their new surroundings is a must, and be sure to ask the breeder any questions you have."

Ginny DeLeon
Broken D Bar Ranch

Preparing Your Family for the New Canine Member

Photo Courtesy of Cindy Jacobson

If your new Miniature Australian Shepherd will be the first dog that your family has owned, there are several topics that you will want to sit down and discuss together. It is important to explain to small children that puppies are delicate and need to be treated very gently. It could be a good idea to spend time with a puppy-owning friend to give your children some experience with puppies before one arrives at your home.

It is also important to prepare your family for the chores that come with owning your new canine companion. It is always a good idea to split up the responsibilities of own-

Photo Courtesy of Carolina Jones

ing a pet. Making a chart is a good way to sort out whose job it is to feed, water, walk, clean up after, and play with the puppy each day. This will help to ensure that your new puppy receives all of the attention and care that it deserves.

If you already have pets, it's important to prepare them for the transition. Rather than introducing your dog to the new puppy all at once, consider using a towel or blanket with the new puppy's scent on it and giving your dog the chance to familiarize itself with its new sibling. It may also be beneficial to have the dogs meet one another in a "neutral" location if your dog has a tendency to be territorial. Finally, it's crucial that you remain calm—your dog has spent a lot of time around you, and it will pick up on your fear and anxiety.

Introduce them gradually and do not let them come into direct contact with the puppy or dog until they seem comfortable. Don't show too much attention to the new family addition, and make sure to include your other pets. Just like children, pets will become jealous of each other if you aren't careful. Sometimes it is helpful to always work with your older pets first. Things like letting them inside before the puppy and feeding them before the puppy have helped mitigate other pet jealous in some situations.

Dangerous Items to Keep Locked Up

"Prepare just like you would for an infant. Put up the things they can get in their mouth and secure cords to make sure they can't pull things down."

Gail Claborn
Circle 5 Aussies

There are many common household items that are dangerous, toxic, or deadly to canines. It is your responsibility as a new pet owner to know what is safe and unsafe for your pet. Some of the most dangerous products in your home are human food, cleaning products, insecticides, and prescription drugs.

Human Foods to Avoid

As much as we want to spoil our pets, it is important to understand that they can't always have what they want. Dogs are known to beg for the delicious human food that we prepare. Some would rather devour it versus eating their pet food. Unfortunately, some of these mouthwatering foods that we as humans enjoy can be incredibly dangerous for our dogs. Below is a list of some of the foods that you should avoid feeding your pet. You'll find more information in Chapter 7.

- Chocolate and coffee: caffeine from these two foods can cause a dog to have heart, kidney, or nervous system problems. Overfeeding a dog chocolate can result in a quick death.

- Grapes: can cause sudden kidney problems or failure in your puppy.

- Onions and garlic: Onions and garlic can cause your dog's red blood cells to burst.

- Avocados: all parts of this fruit are toxic to canines and can cause stomach issues.

*Photo Courtesy of
Cindy Jacobson*

Photo Courtesy of
Christine Nixon

- Alcohol: ethanol in any form of alcohol (beer, wine, champagne, liquor, or even cooking alcohol) is incredibly toxic to dogs and can kill them.

- Xylitol: a new form of sugar substitute present in many foods—it's great for your new diet, but extremely toxic to your dog. Even small amounts can cause hypoglycemia, seizures, or liver failure. Be aware that some peanut butter brands and medications can contain xylitol.

- Meats: you can give your dog meats that have been cooked. It's a good idea to cut them into smaller pieces so that your dog does not choke. You may also need to remove bones that can be become lodged in your dog's throat, especially in poultry. Bird bones are brittle and can splinter into small, sharp pieces.

Cleaning Products & Chemicals to Keep Your Dog Away From:

Household cleaning products are some of the deadliest products in your home. It is important that you keep these items locked up, placed up high where your pet cannot reach them, or in areas that your pet does not frequent. Some of the products that you should keep away from your canine are:

- Bleach
- Laundry Detergent and Dishwashing Pods
- Drain Cleaner
- Oven Cleaner

- Batteries
- Antifreeze
- Fertilizer
- Rodent Killers
- Insect Killers

Preparing an Indoor Space For Your Dog

In all the craziness of preparing for your new Mini Aussie, it can be easy to forget that you need to have a clean, comfortable space that your puppy will be allowed to be in. It is incredibly important to have this space ready before the puppy arrives.

The decision needs to be made whether your puppy will be able to roam the whole house, or if you want to restrict certain areas. You can purchase baby gates to help form boundaries for where the puppy will be able to play and be with family. You will need to make sure the designated area has no dangerous choking hazards and all cabinets are closed so that the puppy does not have access.

You should expect that your puppy will be very inquisitive and want to explore. Early on, you might want to have puppy pads available and keep a close eye on your puppy. You also need to decide where your puppy's food and water bowl will be located. It is best to put these in a non-carpeted area, or near your puppy's sleeping area.

You also have the option of getting a crate for your dog. Some owners worry that crates are like cages that lock their new puppy up, but with the right training, crates actually have the opposite effect. A crate can be a safe, cozy space for your new Mini Aussie, lined with blankets and toys and familiar smells. Feeding your dog inside the crate will cause your dog to form positive associations with the crate, and it can help to avoid messy nights while you potty train your new pup.

Preparing Outside Spaces

HELPFUL TIP
Be Prepared!

Like very young children, your puppy needs your protection. Begin "puppy proofing" before your new companion comes home. Miniature Australian Shepherds will "scope the perimeter" of their new environment, oftentimes getting into mischief or harm. Be proactive by removing household chemicals, electrical cords, and tempting indoor plants. Keep interior doors closed to avoid having your puppy fall downstairs or enter rooms that are off-limits. Do not leave your Mini Aussie home alone in the house for extended periods of time. This intelligent animal needs daily activity and mental stimulation to avoid becoming ill-tempered and unsociable. A busy, active Mini Aussie is a happy companion.

Whether or not your puppy will primarily be an indoor or outdoor pet, you will need to pay equal attention to preparing your pet's space. There are many dangers that may be located in your yard. Make sure your fencing is free from holes, jagged boards, or metal. Puppies like to explore and find escape routes. If you do not have fencing, be prepared to keep your puppy on a leash so it does not run out into the street or escape.

You will need to make sure that your puppy's outdoor play area is free of any harmful items or debris. First, pick up any small rocks or pieces of wood that your puppy could choke or swallow. Then you will need to make sure that your lawn is mowed so that insects such as fleas and ticks do not proliferate. If you are going to spray for insects or weeds, you need to do it a few weeks before your pet arrives home. It may also be a good idea to research any plants or trees that are located in your yard, to make sure they are not toxic to your pup.

Some examples of toxic plants include:
- Aloe
- Azaleas
- Hibiscus
- Fruits such as apricots or apples
- Nightshade
- Birds of Paradise

In addition to making sure your yard is safe for your new Mini Aussie, you should also make sure your yard has ample shade, a source of water, and that your dog won't be in a high-traffic area where other dogs or careless passersby may cause injury to your pup. Before your puppy comes home, you will need to make sure that you have the following items:
- Pet food bowl
- Puppy food that is recommended by your breeder
- Pet water bowl
- Crate or dog bed
- Newspapers or puppy pads
- Puppy toys
- Dog gate (if you do not have a crate)
- Gentle puppy shampoo

CHAPTER 4
Bringing Your Miniature Australian Shepherd Home

"Transitioning a new puppy into your home can be stressful on the puppy. Try not to drastically change everything in its life. Ask the breeder where they were kept and try to setup a place similar. Ask for a blanket or something that smells like its previous home to make the transition more comfortable. Spend lots of time with your new puppy as this will help it bond to you."

Robert Kidd
Kidd's Toy Aussies

Transporting Your Dog

When bringing your new pup home, either by car or by plane, it is important to make sure that your dog is safe and secure. Your pup may be nervous or uncomfortable in these new environments, and you should do everything you can to help them remain calm.

Make sure your pup is properly buckled in with a doggy seat belt, in a crate, or otherwise secured. If you have blankets and toys for your puppy, consider placing these in the car or crate with your dog so that they will be familiar. If you have small children, make sure to talk with them beforehand about staying calm and not roughhousing with the puppy until it gets settled in—you want your Mini Aussie to feel safe with you and your family, not terrified!

When you arrive home, it can be tempting to let your new pup roam free. Instead, you should introduce it to the crate or space that you have created for it, and make sure that this is designated as a safe space for your new pup. Remember that after being in the car or a plane for a long period of time, your pup will probably need to use the bathroom! Give it some time outside to take care of business before bringing it into the house.

However, always be aware of putting them down in unknown areas. Until they are fully vaccinated, they are at risk for deadly pathogens, like parvovirus. You will not be able to see if the virus or bacteria is in the grass, so setting them down only in places that you know no infected dogs have been is very important.

The First Night Home

You need to have a plan in place for your puppy's first night at home. The first night can be very difficult for both of you. Your puppy will be in a new environment, away from its mother and siblings while it sleeps. It may whine, scratch, or bark. By now you should have decided whether or not your puppy will sleep in a crate, on a dog bed, or near you.

If you have chosen to place your puppy in a crate at night there are a few things to keep in mind. You should expect your puppy to yelp and howl as soon as you are out of sight. The good thing about a crate is that your puppy is contained and cannot get into any harmful situations or dangerous products around your home.

Before placing your puppy inside of the crate, ensure that you assembled your crate properly so it doesn't collapse or come apart. Make sure that the crate is the right size for your dog, giving it enough

Photo Courtesy of
Stephanie Mendoza

space to stand and turn around without being overly spacious. Place a soft mat or blanket inside the front of the crate so your pup has a soft and warm place to lie down. In the back of the crate, place either newspapers or puppy pads down in case your puppy needs to relieve itself during the night. Keeping your new family member warm, dry, and comfortable will help you have a more enjoyable first night. This should all be ready to go prior to your pup's first night home.

If you have chosen to let your new Miniature Australian Shepherd puppy sleep in a puppy bed, you may be in for a more challenging night. While a dog bed is comfortable for a puppy, expect to be constantly placing the little scamp back into the bed, as they will prefer to curl up next to you. You

Photo Courtesy of Anna-Marie Gooch

will also have to worry about the puppy wandering off when you fall asleep. This can be a problem if your puppy gets into any household substances that are lying around, needs to use the bathroom during the night, or decides to shred your new pair of slippers.

You and your family may want to discuss an arrangement for letting your new pup outside during the night so that it has a chance to use the bathroom outside. You can take turns, set an alarm for specific times during the night, or listen for your pup's whining, but it is important to remember that you should not get out of bed to comfort your dog every time it barks or yelps. Your Mini Aussie will need time to adjust to its new home, and comforting it each time it makes a noise will encourage it to be noisy during the night rather than going to sleep. It may seem cruel to ignore your new pup, knowing it may be lonely or confused, but a firm hand is just as important as a loving one.

Choosing a Veterinarian and the First Vet Visit

One of the most important decisions that you make for your Mini Aussie will be choosing a veterinarian. If you have had other dogs in the past and already have an established relationship with a local veterinarian, then you are on the right path. However, if this is your first puppy, there are ways to find the right vet for you and your dog.

When looking for a veterinarian, consider asking other dog owners near you, the shelter you adopted from, or the breeder that you purchased your dog from for recommendations. Another way to research veterinarians is to look online. It is important to make sure that your veterinarian is American Animal Hospital Association (AAHA) certified. By making sure that they are accredited, you will assure that your pet is getting a high level of care.

QUOTE
Caveat Emptor
(Buyer Beware)

According to the AKC, being a dog owner is an expensive undertaking. Akc.org asserts that small- to medium-sized dogs with lifespans of between 13-15 years will cost their owners upward of $15, 000 over their lifetime. You may do well to ask yourself, "Should I purchase pet insurance for my dog?" With an abundance of policies and premiums available, be aware of what you are paying for and what may or may not be included in your dog's health policy if you choose to purchase pet health insurance. Inquire with your dog's breeder, your veterinarian, and search online with trusted organizations like the AKC to examine the wide range of insurance policies that will fit your pet's needs and your pocketbook.

*Photo Courtesy of
Lindsey Creal*

What To Expect at Your First Vet Visit

Once you locate a vet, it is important that you set up an appointment according to the breeder's records of when the next set of shots are due for your puppy. Be ready for the first visit to take longer, as the veterinarian will want to have you fill out papers in order to get a medical background on record. Your vet will more than likely do some of the following things:

- Listen to your puppy's heart
- Weigh your puppy
- Do a fecal test to check for parasites
- Give any needed vaccinations
- Check the puppy's ears, nose, mouth, and eyes
- Check the puppy for fleas and ticks

Your vet may consult with you about the right pet foods for your puppy. They should be able to recommend a good nutrition and exercise program for your new family member. They may also give you free samples of different products to use and your new pup's vaccination schedule.

There is a lot to consider when choosing a vet. You want professional care and a friendly disposition, but you should also check what kind of care plans your vet offers (some provide memberships or monthly packages that will give you steep discounts on medicine and checkups) and whether or not they have emergency hours.

Always make sure you have an emergency plan for your new puppy. Just like you probably know which hospital is closest to you, you should also be aware of where you can take your dog in an emergency.

Puppy Classes

Puppy classes can be a great way for you to bond with your new Miniature Australian Shepherd. Puppy classes are geared toward different age ranges, so you should be able to find one that is appropriate for your new family member no matter what stage of life it is in. These classes can help your family learn to bond properly with your puppy or help it to socialize with other puppies and dogs.

Puppy classes can also help you get your puppy on the right track to early obedience training. Class instructors can help you teach your puppy basic commands, how to walk on a leash, etc. These skills will be crucial for you and your puppy for years to come. You can find puppy classes at some local pet retailers, which should have schedules listed on their websites. You should also be able to do online research to find other classes near you from professional trainers, who are usually more knowledgeable.

Mini Aussies are highly intelligent and can be very easy to train. The downside is that they are often mischievous or test boundaries—your new puppy is sure to have a lot of personality, so be sure to outline behavioral goals in advance and stick with them.

Cost Breakdown for the First Year

Having a pet is expensive. Not only do you need the money to buy your new puppy or dog, but you have to be able to pay for its everyday care. On top of that, you may come across unanticipated expenses, such as emergency veterinary visits or doggy daycare when you are out of town.

Photo Courtesy of
Carolina Jones

*Photo Courtesy of
Jackie Govert*

Here is a rough outline of annual pet expenses, which can vary wide-ly by location:

Food: $120+

Annual Medical Exams: $235

Toys and Treats: $55

License: $15

Pet Health Insurance: $225

Miscellaneous: $45+

Total Annual Costs: $695+

According to a report from Money Under 30, (cite source better) the to-tal first-year cost of owning a dog could be around $1,270.

CHAPTER 5
Being a Puppy Parent

"With all Aussies, both adults and puppies, the first few weeks will be a transition period. Don't be surprised if they don't eat much at first, and don't get frustrated if they have accidents at first. Aussies are very intelligent, so it shouldn't take long for them to learn the new routine and new settings."

Cayla Cox
CC Miniature and Toy Australian Shepherds

Setting Expectations

Becoming a new owner to a Miniature Australian Shepherd can be very exciting. Thinking of names, picking out toys, getting special treats, and imagining the things you will do with your puppy is lots of fun! But just like becoming a new parent to a human baby, there is a lot to consider. It is important that you decide what your goals are from the very beginning.

The first thing to understand is that you need to set realistic goals and expectations for both you and your new puppy. For example, you may be all for training your puppy, thinking that it will be the next star on America's Got Talent or the next movie star. But let's face it. The dog may not even know its own name yet, so slow down.

Some possible realistic goals and expectations would be:
- Teaching basic manners
- Not getting frustrated with potty training
- Beginning to socialize your dog
- Introducing your puppy to the veterinarian

Curbing Unwanted Behavior

"Mini Aussies are natural herders and tend to be a little mouthy. You need to redirect that behavior to a toy. It's never ok for them to nip at you."

Gail Claborn
Circle 5 Aussies

Once you become a dog owner, you will definitely notice that your new family member comes with some bad habits. Dogs have instincts that aren't always polite, especially in mixed company. It will be your job to attempt to curb these behaviors in your new Miniature Australian Shepherd and teach them your expectations in the home.

Begging

Don't be surprised if your Mini Aussie puppy snubs its food every now and again if it smells human food cooking. Begging for food is a common complaint with any pet dog, and who wouldn't rather have a juicy steak instead of dog food? The key is not to give in to those sad eyes that will stare into your soul!

Dogs beg in several different ways. Some dogs will simply stare at you hoping to get a bite of food from your plate. Others will be even less polite and jump up, put their paws on your lap or table, and take what they want. They may also persistently whine, much like a toddler or child.

It is important to correct this behavior early on. Human food is generally not a balanced diet for your dog. Sure, a piece of meat every now and again isn't going to hurt anything, but it is just better for your dog's overall health to keep them on their regular food.

Photo Courtesy of Erynne Johnson

Miniature Australian Shepherds tend to be a breed that likes to be in your space, so more than likely, you will face this challenge at some point with your dog.

There are several ways to get your dog to stop this behavior. An easy tip to curb begging is to make sure your dog is fed before your family mealtime. This way the dog will have already eaten and be full when you are enjoying your meal.

Another alternative is to just win the staring contest with your pooch. No matter how much they stare at you during your meal, DO NOT make eye contact back. Eventually your dog will get the hint that you are not going to give them anything from the table, and that their attempts are futile.

It is always better to avoid feeding your dog from the table at all, but for those who simply can't resist making it a habit, try waiting until your meal is finished, and then place the food in the dog's bowl. Make sure not to encourage your dog to linger around the table, as it can grow tiresome and be frustrating when you have guests.

Digging

Some dogs just love to dig, and as an energy dog, Miniature Australian Shepherds are no exception. If they are outside the majority of the time, they will sometimes find a dirt patch and go to town when bored. Watch that the spot they choose isn't near a fence or other barrier, that they could tunnel under to freedom!

HELPFUL TIP
A Proper Puppy Parent

Miniature Australian Shepherds were bred to herd livestock, oftentimes resorting to nipping at the heels of sheep or cattle to keep them in line. If your Mini Aussie isn't properly trained and diligently exercised, he may well transfer this herding behavior to children, other pets, or even bikes and cars! It is up to the "puppy parent" to keep this bright and energetic dog occupied with challenging tasks to keep the mind and body occupied. Decide what your goals are for your new pet. Miniature Aussies have been successfully trained for search and rescue, hearing dogs, and even therapy dogs.

It is important to understand there are instinctive reasons why dogs dig. For example, in hot weather, dogs dig to get to damp dirt to cool themselves by lying in the depression. Dogs will also dig if they smell rodents underground, such as a mole or gopher, in an attempt to catch the varmint.

There are a few ways to break your dog of the digging

habit. If your dog is digging be-cause it is getting too warm, you need to help it find another way to cool off. Make sure that it has a shaded area and cool, fresh water to drink. You can also get your dog a plastic pool com-monly sold for human children in stores during the summer. They will love splashing around!

Photo Courtesy of Haley Sullivan

If your dog is after vermin, you can deter it from digging by dealing with your rodent prob-lem. Setting traps is an easy way to catch moles and gophers, but you will need to make sure that your pet does not have access to the area when the traps are active. You can also put out rodent bait. If you use this method, be extremely cautious. You must keep your dog away from bait and poisons, as ingestion of these products can be fatal in canines.

If you keep your pet outdoors and it is digging out of its enclosure, there are ways to keep your dog safely inside. One way, if your dog is in a small-er space, is to get a cattle panel and create a floor to the bottom of the pen. The dog will still be able to dig within the squares, but not out. If your dog is running the length of your yard, however, you will need to find places near the fence where your dog is digging and place deterrents in the area. There are a variety of products available, ranging from chemical sprays to phys-ical barriers.

Unwanted Noise

Dogs employ a wide array sounds, depending on the situation. For ex-ample, they growl when they feel threatened. A dog will whine when it is anxious, excited, or wants something. They may vocalize because they hear noises that are unfamiliar--like sirens-- they are lonely or they are respond-ing to wildlife, such as coyotes.

A certain level of noise is to be expected from any dog, but when it's ex-cessive or unwarranted, there are different methods to stop it. Try ignoring your dog when they are whining or barking for attention. If they realize that making noise will not obtain the desired result, oftentimes they will stop.

Photo Courtesy of Cindy Jacobson

Another way to quiet barking is to very sternly tell them no. Some pets are obedient enough that they will want to please you and cease what they are doing.

So what do you do when these methods do not stop your dog from making noise?

Luckily, there are several new higher tech of addressing the problem. Some send out a high-pitched, unpleasant frequency each time a dog barks. Handheld versions can be used not only to address barking issues, but for other unwanted behaviors, like digging and aggression.

Another option is an electric collar, which gives the dog a slight electric pulse. Many also have sound only settings, without the physical reinforcement. This device will often work when others won't. They should not be used to punish a dog, but rather to curtail unwanted behaviors that your dog is exhibiting. Many offer a handheld remote that will give a dog a warning beep before a charge is issued, so that your dog has the chance to self-correct. Some collars can also be on an automatic setting to prevent bad behavior from your dog while you are not present.

Consider obedience training as an option if you are having difficulty controlling your dog's barking—Mini Aussies have a tendency to bark at strangers, so socializing them well or simply blocking their view of the street can both be effective ways to combat excessive noise.

Chewing

When dogs are young, they go through a phase called "teething," during which they will chew on everything they can find! To puppies, the world is completely new. They are like toddlers who want to touch everything and put it in their mouths, hungry or not. They will chew on things because it feels good on their gums or use chewing as a form of play when bored.

Canines will also chew when they become anxious. A dog may get nervous in a car if it associates car rides with going to the vet. Taking a favorite toy along helps to alleviate this anxiety. Because your pup may be anxious when you leave for school, work, or to simply enjoy the town, addressing your dog's chewing issues may prevent you from coming home to find your trash gone through, your couch cushions or pillows shredded, or your favorite expensive pair of shoes destroyed.

There are several different ways that you can keep your dog from chewing on objects that are in your home. The best thing that you can do is to keep your dog from becoming bored. Try to spend more time playing with your dog and giving him the attention he craves. This is especially true if he's the only dog.

Taking your dog for long walks and making sure that he has plenty of exercise is a great way to combat boredom. You can also take him to a lo-

Photo Courtesy of Taylor Hall

cal dog park or allow him to run free in your fenced yard for extended periods of time. If neither of these is an option, just spend time throwing a ball, stick, or other object to your dog and playing games. This will help to keep him mentally stimulated.

Giving your dog chewing items that are "ok" to be chewed on is also helpful. Toys can range from balls, ropes, stuffed animals, special dog toys, and different types of bones. Once your dog has designated items to chew on, he will be more likely to leave human items alone.

Playtime & Bonding

Making sure your puppy gets ample time to play is crucial to its development. Playtime helps your puppy to develop mentally and physically. It also helps your puppy to bond with you and other pets in your home. Playtime can be used as a reward as well.

When you play with your dog, you will want to use certain types of toys to keep them entertained. Dogs who have a tendency to destroy or chew through toys, for example, may enjoy a more durable chew toy, that can bounce and roll around. You can also place treats inside of some of this type of toy and as the dog plays with it, it will release them slowly for their efforts. This encourages your dog to be more active and will keep them entertained for a longer period of time.

If you are a more high-tech person and enjoy using the latest technology, you can also find electronic or automatic toys that will roll around or bounce on the floor to keep your puppy happily chasing them. Others allow you to use a remote control or your smartphone to get in on the fun while manipulating the smart toy. These toys often come in the shapes of bones or balls. The smart toys are made to stay durable, safe, and are able to be cleaned. The only downside of interactive dog toys is that they are a bit pricey, but if your pup loves to play, the cost may be well worth it!

Other more traditional types of toys are ropes, stuffed squeaking toys, and balls. These toys are much more economical. You can buy more of them, or replace them more often for a fraction of the price. Puppies love to carry around or tug toy ropes. A traditional tennis ball is a toy that can't be overlooked either. Puppies love to interact with you as you throw a ball to them. Puppies also enjoy chasing, chewing, and shaking stuffed squeak toys. Many puppies will get attached to a particular one, just like a human child will. This will become their comfort toy that they do not want to be without.

At the end of the day, the toys you purchase for your Mini Aussie will serve as a bonding tool. By setting aside a playtime every day, he will learn to view you as a friend and companion.

Leaving Your Dog At Home Alone

"Australian Shepherds are intensely loyal and social, when they leave their litters they will look to their new owners as the pack leader while they find their place in the world. Leaving them alone for extended periods of time during this period can cause separation anxiety and they may cause damage to the home or themselves if not safely confined."

Ashley Bryan
Ashley's Aussies

Eventually, you will have to leave your dog at home alone. This will more than likely be hard on both you and your puppy. Puppies can get anxiety from being separated from you, as you have become the replacement for their mother. But your absence does not have to be a traumatic experience.

Puppies need to learn that if you leave, you will also return. It's best to leave them alone for no more than an hour the first few times that you venture away. For example, you can make a quick visit to the grocery store or to run other errands. Your puppy may yelp while you are gone, but he will then see that you do return. If you have to be away longer, it may be a good idea to arrange for a neighbor or relative to come let him out regularly so he can relieve himself and stretch his legs.

Some dogs may be left outside when you are away. If you have an enclosed backyard with a sturdy fence, puppies may enjoy being outside on a nice warm day. If you are going to leave your puppy outside, you do need to make sure that if rain or a storm comes up, they have a doghouse to retreat into to get out of the weather. Being outside offers your puppy a chance to be less stressed and for you to not have to clean up any messes when you return home.

Crate training your dog has many benefits. Having a safe environment helps puppies feel more at home. It also keeps them from destroying your household objects by acting out or having an accident on the carpet. A crate can be their comfort if you let them keep their favorite toy or blanket with them. Crates also help to keep your puppy out of dangerous chemicals or objects that may be within their reach.

When you do come home, you and your new pup will certainly be excited to see one another. However, remember your behavioral standards! If your dog tries to jump on you or barks excessively, consider telling them to sit or wait for them to stop barking before you lavish them with attention, otherwise you may encourage those behaviors. You don't want to make a fuss about leaving or returning home, as excessive rituals can contribute to your dog developing separation anxiety.

Once you figure out a regular routine with your dog, it will become much easier on both of you. Remember, there will come a time when both of you will be more relaxed about your coming and going. It may be hard to leave your new puppy, but it is part of life that you will both adapt to.

Bedtime Routine

When you first get your puppy, your odds of sleeping through the night are comparable to having a new baby at home. If you eventually want to have a normal sleep pattern, you will have to train your dog to adhere as closely to your sleeping schedule as possible. Dogs can adjust to routines as long as you keep as close to the same schedule as possible.

One way to begin establishing a nighttime routine with your Miniature Australian Shepherd is to have set times that you go to bed. For example, if you go to bed one night at 8 p.m. and then the next night you go to bed at midnight, your puppy will be confused. This could have him waking you up wanting to play in the middle of the night instead of resting. Instead, you should really try to go to bed at close to the same time each night. If you go to bed at 8 p.m., try and keep to that time frame as much as possible.

Getting your puppy to sleep at the right time can often pose problems. One thing you can do is to play with him right before bedtime. If a puppy plays extremely hard, it will be exhausted and usually be ready to fall asleep. Another thing that you can do is quiet yourself and your household down. A puppy will not fall asleep if there are a lot of things going on or a lot of noise around it. If it is given a quiet environment, a puppy will drift off to sleep much more easily.

There are a few methods that you can use to keep your puppy asleep longer in between times that it needs to go out during the night. You can make sure that there is a ticking clock in the room where the puppy is sleeping. This is a soothing sound for most dogs. You can also leave a radio playing soft music. Lastly, you can look up heartbeat sounds on the Internet. This often puts puppies that have just left their mothers to sleep, because they find comfort from the familiar sound.

Whether you have crate trained your new puppy or not, you will want to make sure and develop a consistent food schedule before bedtime. It is not unusual for a puppy to need to use the bathroom 30 minutes after consuming food or water. For this reason, refrain from letting your puppy eat or drink after his final bathroom visit before bedtime. You should also make sure that you give your puppy adequate time to empty his bowels and bladder outside right before bed. You may be tired, but don't rush him!

Set an alarm for every few hours to take your puppy back out. Puppies do not have the capacity to hold their bodily functions like grown dogs do. These time frames will get further and further apart as your dog grows. Eventually, you will not have to get up during the night at all, but until then, you will have to make the effort to tend to your puppy's needs.

CHAPTER 6
Housetraining and Enclosures

"It is very important to keep the dog or puppy on a routine (go outside when they first wake up, right after they eat, and periodically in between, etc). Our adult Aussies are free to roam in the house, but for puppies, crate training tends to work well because they try not to use the potty where they sleep."

Cayla Cox
CC Miniature and Toy Australian Shepherds

One of the first things you should do when you arrive home with your new puppy is to take it directly to the area that you hope that it will utilize as its bathroom. Wherever you choose to let your puppy go now, make sure that it is a place that you will not have a problem with him going as he grows older.

Options for Potty Training

There are several methods of potty training a new puppy. Some of the more popular methods are crate training, outdoor training, pad training, and paper training. There are pros and cons to each approach. The table below explains this.

Photo Courtesy of
Stephannie Mendoza

Method	Pros	Cons
Crate training	• Knowing that while you are away, your pet will not mess where it shouldn't. • Teaches your dog to control their bowels more quickly. • Dogs learn to feel safe inside their crate. • Great if you live in a warm or mild climate.	• Leaving your dog inside of a crate too long can result in destructive behaviors. • If you do not get the right size of crate, your dog may feel too confined. • It can be dangerous if the cage is not assembled properly. • You must clean out the crate when accidents happen.
Outdoor training	• After you get your pet trained, there will be no messy clean-up. • You can teach your pet the command "Go potty!" and they will understand. • No supervision if you have an enclosed yard. • Great if you live in a warm or mild climate.	• After you get your pet trained, there will be no messy clean-up. • You can teach your pet the command "Go potty!" and they will understand. • No supervision if you have an enclosed yard. • Great if you live in a warm or mild climate.
Pad or paper training or indoor grass pads	• Great for small dogs. • More comfortable if you live in a cold climate. • Simpler if you live in apartment buildings where you cannot get to an outside area quickly.	• Not so great for large dogs. • Both puppy pads and newspapers can become expensive. • Improper placement can cause some rather gross situations. • Dogs may choose to tear the pads or newspapers up.

Crate Training

"Aussies have a high level of intelligence and problem solving skills. Crate-training, house-training and obedience-training can sometimes only takes a few days (for owners who are willing to put the intensive work in as soon as they bring their puppy home)."

Ashley Bryan
Ashley's Aussies

Crate training is one of the best options for housebreaking your dog. There are various reasons that to recommend this method. Puppies tend to find safe places when they move to new homes. Giving them a crate with a blanket and their favorite toy will make them soon feel at home. The crate will become a place where they are at peace.

To crate train your new puppy, you will need to purchase a crate. Make sure that the crate is the right size that will still accommodate your Miniature Australian Shepherd as it grows or you will have to buy a bigger one later on down the road. It is also important that you do your research on which crates are the safest and sturdiest for your puppy. Selecting the right crate will have a lot to do with the success that you have while crate training your pup.

Photo Courtesy of
Amanda Akagi

It is advisable to put their favorite toy inside of the crate with them, along with a soft blanket. The two objects can provide comfort to the dog, much like a young child finds comfort in their favorite teddy bear and blanket. You may also want to put a radio in the room and turn it very low on a station with soft music. This will help to soothe the puppy.

The first few times you place your puppy in the crate it is to be expected that they will howl, whine, bark, or make other noises protesting being inside of the crate. It will be hard, but you need to leave them for at least an hour by themselves inside of the crate. Eventually they will calm down. Once they have been inside of the crate for an hour, take them outside and let them relieve themselves. Every 3 days, increase the amount of time that you leave them inside of the crate by 30 minutes. This will help to train their bladder and bowels to hold themselves for the allocated amount of time.

HELPFUL TIP
You Can Teach an Old Dog New Tricks!

Whether you have purchased a puppy or an older dog, you can successfully house-train your pet if you are dedicated to the task. Old and young dogs alike often "sneak off" to do their business inside the house. Watch carefully for this behavior and take the dog out immediately before an accident occurs. Inside areas that have been used often require thorough cleaning and disinfecting to remove the smell of urine and feces. Your veterinarian will be able to advise you on a safe product that has been specially formulated to remove pet odors without harming your dog. Keep to a regular schedule for walks at least three to five times daily or more as necessary while house-training your Mini Aussie.

Instinctively, puppies will not want to make a mess where they sleep. This is part of what helps them hold their bladders and waste. However, you must remember that they are puppies and, if you are not diligent in sticking to a schedule, accidents will happen. If the puppy does have an accident you will need to clean up the mess and sanitize the crate using a pet-safe cleaner.

Remember; avoid using the crate as a mechanism for punishing your dog. It should be a safe, comfortable place, free of negative associations. That way, when you leave the house, your dog will not be anxious while stuck inside!

Photo Courtesy of
Mariel García

Outdoor Training

Outdoor training can be a very beneficial method for some Miniature Australian Shepherd owners. It is great for those who have access to a front yard, back yard, or those who live in the country. It is not necessarily conducive to pet owners who live in an apartment.

With outdoor training, there is less mess in the long run. You won't have to deal with dirty doggy pads or toss soiled newspapers if your dog is trained to go outdoors. Or be out the expense of them. You also don't have to be anxious about them destroying your home on the inside.

To outdoor train your dog, you need to always take the puppy out the same door each time. For example, if you are allowing your dog to use your backyard to go to the restroom, then you need to always take him out the back door or door that leads to the yard. This will help your puppy to know that the door is a way to get to the potty. The idea is that eventually your puppy will go to the door and either paw at it or whimper to indicate that he needs to be let out. Some owners alternatively teach their dogs to bump bells hanging on a string from the door knob with their paw or nose.

You may also want to install a doggy door so your dog can let itself out during the day. A doggy door is a great tool when you can't constantly be around to let your pet in and out or don't want to be inconvenienced by taking them outdoors.

A downside of doggy doors is that they can be somewhat difficult to install, requiring professional tools, and sometimes a hole be cut into a door or wall. However, newer models exist that are easier to install and can often be done in a snap by a handy homeowner. Another drawback is that your puppy may also decide to drag things inside from the yard that you'd rather not be in your house. Or, there's a chance a bold wild animal can march right into your home if they wander into the yard.

If you plan on outdoor training your dog, it is paramount that you decide on what command you will use, and use only that word or phrase consistently. Common commands are, "Go potty," "go pee," "go bathroom," or "wet" to remind them of the reason that they are outdoors. Again, whatever you choose to say, use the exact same command each time. Consistency is key.

Puppies are notorious for becoming distracted and forgetting they even needed to go potty. One way to encourage your puppy use the bathroom more quickly outside is to purchase a spray attractant that helps them know exactly where you would like them to do their business in your yard. Or, visit a spot you know other dogs, especially ones from your same household, frequent.

Puppies will usually choose the same area time after time to use as a bathroom, so if you don't want them going at the foot of the porch, guide them toward another location right off.

When working on potty training, don't distract your puppy when it is going. The slightest distraction could cause them to stop too early, such as with urination, and then once back inside, they will finish going in the house when the distraction is over. You should also never abruptly stop them from relieving themselves outside, but make sure they have fully emptied themselves.

Outdoor training offers a more natural approach to potty training for your Miniature Australian Shepherd. It all depends on what your living situation is. There is less mess, and can be an easy option to teach your pup to eliminate.

Pad & Paper Training

If you do not have an outdoor space for your dog to use the facilities on, you may want to look into pad or paper training your new family member. Pad or paper training can be a more convenient option if you do not have access to a yard or other grassy area. The cleanup can be easy, but you may not like the smell that it can leave in your home. Paper and pad training can also be relatively expensive in the long run.

Training your dog to use pads or paper can be a difficult chore, but there are many products on the market that can help you make the transition easier. You may, for example, use a urine-scented spray that triggers your puppy to recognize that the pad or paper is where they need to do their business. Puppies instinctually go to the bathroom where other dogs have gone before, so you can simply spritz it onto your puppy pads or paper and your puppy will willingly go to them to use the bathroom.

There are also turf pads. These pads have artificial grass that simulate a more natural environment to potty your pup. Because dogs instinctively prefer grassy areas, the success rate seems to be higher in getting your pup to choose to use the spot. Turf pads also offer an easier cleanup using dish soap and water. Because they are reusable, artificial turf pads are also more economical in the long run, than many disposable options.

Another option is to order fresh patches of grass for your dog. Yes, these are actual patches of real grass that your dog can go on while inside of your house or apartment! These patches are incredibly convenient and you can toss them once they have been used. Though cleanup is easy and dogs often take to this method very readily, real turf can be expensive.

If you are interested in genuine turf for your puppy, you can usually set up an automatic renewal plan with a company that ships, and they will send you fresh patches on a regular basis. Some dog owners have also found local sources, such a turf companies or seasonally in some home improvement stores or lumber yards, that allow pickup.

Once you decide which indoor product you want to use to train your puppy, you will need to establish a routine in order to house train them. The best method is to choose a confined area, such as the laundry room or patio, to place the pad or paper. Start guiding your puppy toward the pad or paper about 15 minutes after he eats or drinks.

After he has consumed a meal or liquid, bring your puppy to the confined area that they are expected to relieve themselves in. Every few minutes bring your puppy directly over to the pad or paper and let them sniff it. If you have used the attractant or are using one of the turf types, the puppy should get the idea. If the puppy tries to play instead of paying attention, gently keep placing it's nose back on the spot to encourage sniffing.

You should give a verbal command when trying to get your puppy to use the pads or paper, just as you would in outdoor training. Eventually, they will associate the phrase with the action, and should relieve themselves on cue.

But at first, when the puppy goes in the right spot–on command or not— immediately praise him for going in the correct place. If you stay consistent your puppy should soon get the right idea.

Photo Courtesy of
Judy Bramwell

The First Few Weeks

"Miniature Australian Shepherds are extremely easy to train. Predictability and consistency are the keys. And start early, as soon as your puppy comes home. Eight week old puppies can be house trained, crate trained and obedience trained. You just have to put the work in."

Ashley Bryan
Ashley's Aussies

Potty training your new Miniature Australian Shepherd is much like potty training a toddler. It is not easy. It is not fast. It will frustrate you, and at some point you will probably want to give up. Successfully house training your dog can take as little as a few weeks or as long as several months, depending on the dog.

The first few weeks that you have your puppy, it will be important that you create a routine for him. You will need to have a set schedule of when he is given food and water. The reasoning behind this is that usually, about 20-30 minutes after a dog consumes a meal, it will need to go to the restroom. If you set your feeding schedule around the times that you will be home, there should be fewer surprise accidents while you are away at work, school, or somewhere else.

It is important that you familiarize yourself with your dog's bathroom behaviors and signals. You will have to watch your puppy like a hawk for the first few weeks during potty training in order to catch the cues that your new puppy needs to relieve itself. One of the things that a puppy will do when it needs to go to the bathroom is sniff the area for the perfect place. They will usually go in a circle when sniffing to indicate they are about to go.

If you notice your puppy has begun sniffing, you need to be on the alert. This is especially true if the puppy is returning to an area that they have previously wet on or soiled. It may be a false alarm, since puppies are naturally curious and like to sniff new smells, but it is always a good idea to take them outdoors or place them on a puppy pad anyway, just in case.

You will also need to keep a close eye on your puppy while he is playing. Just like a child who gets too occupied with what they are doing and ignores their bladder or bowels signals, a puppy can get too involved in the game. Puppies sometimes wait too long to go and simply won't be able to hold it any longer.

Rewarding Positive Behavior

It is vital that you reward your puppy any time they do well in their bathroom training. If you praise your dog, he will be more likely to repeat the desired behavior. After all, a dog wants to please his owner!

Let your dog have a treat each time it relieves itself in the desired spot. If your pooch receives a food reward each time, it will gladly go to the bathroom just to get the treat.

There are many pre-packaged treats that you may choose to give your pup. You may also want to get a cookie jar and bake your own homemade treats. You can also give your dog a chew or canine-approved bone, as that will keep them occupied for quite some time afterward. Just make sure that you do not give them too much and spoil their supper.

Another idea to reward your puppy is to give it extra outdoor playtime. Mini Aussies are an extremely energetic breed that loves to run outside, jump, and play, and will relish the opportunity to have some fun! If you are using the outdoor method to potty train, you can let him run around longer once he has gone. You could also get a ball, Frisbee, or other suitable outdoor toy. Puppies love the attention and getting to play with their owners any chance they get. A game is a worthy reward for any pooch!

Room to Roam

If you do not want to give your dog free run of your house during the potty training phase, a good way to allow them a safe space to play is to purchase a dog playpen, often called an exercise pen or ex pen. Easily found online or in most pet stores, they provide a small portable boundary to prevent your dog from wandering off or getting into things it shouldn't be into.

Playpens come in different sizes and styles, and are as individualistic as your needs. They are also useful post house training, such as if you are having company over. They can be effective for quarantining your dog from guests. If your home contains a large number of breakable objects, or if there are places you want to prevent your dog from getting into, playpens can be a great way to break up the space in your house and limit your dog's freedom without cooping them up in a crate.

For a more permanent safe space you can leave a dog to roam in unattended, look into larger dog kennels, which typically are 5' X 5' or 5' X 10'.

Because Mini Aussies are such an energetic breed, doggy doors can be another way for your pup to exercise itself, yet still have indoor access. For a breed that needs extra stimulation, this can be a lifesaver. They can also be a safety feature for your pet in the event of fire or bad weather, allowing them to escape dangerous conditions.

If you opt to buy a doggy door for outdoor access while you are away, you need to understand that they are meant to be used with fenced properties. A Miniature Australian Shepherd could easily run off, get into a something that they are not supposed to, get on a busy road with cars, or be stolen by a passerby.

Whether you choose to buy a playpen, kennel or a doggy door for your pup to have a bit of extra room to stretch its legs, it is important that you understand that neither is meant to act as an excuse to neglect your pet. Yes, we all have jobs and social engagements that we need to attend, but a pet cannot be left at home unable to socialize. Apathy or lack of care can cause your pet to become destructive, poorly behaved, or aggressive.

CHAPTER 7
Food and Nutrition

"When first bringing home your Mini Aussie it is important to have a bag of the food that the puppy is currently eating. If you plan to switch foods, mix the new and old food together (half-and-half) over a period of several weeks instead of just switching foods immediately. Switching the puppy's diet immediately can upset the puppy's stomach and cause it to have unnecessary accidents in its kennel or in the house."

Ashley Bryan
Ashley's Aussies

Types of Dog Food

Choosing a quality dog food is important for your dog's health and happiness. Dog foods come in different types. There is the traditional dog kibble or dry dog food. Kibble usually consists of small shaped pieces or crunchy dog food. Companies have managed to create a wide range of flavors to tempt your pet's palate. Dog kibble usually comes inside of different-sized bags or buckets.

Another type of dog food that is available is wet dog food. Wet dog food is traditionally known as canned dog food. However, today's market has provided newer versions that can be found in the freezer section among human food. Canned dog food can come as chunks of fresh meat mixed with gravy or vegetables. It can also come in a more condensed form that resembles a solid chunk of meat.

Some dog foods are specifically made for dogs during different stages of their lives. Puppy chows or formulas are made just for puppies aging from 6 weeks to 18 months of age. These foods are important because they provide growing puppies with the nutrients they need to grow and thrive. There are also dog foods that cater to adult dogs. Adult dogs need different nutrition than a growing puppy. These dog foods tend to be higher in protein in order to keep your dog active and energetic.

There are also specialized types of dog foods for dogs that have reached their senior years in life. Senior dog foods usually contain ingredients that help your dog with their bones, teeth, and joints. As your dog grows older, it will start to lose bone density and be less flexible. Senior dogs may also need smaller bits of food to help keep their teeth healthy. These dog foods generally provide more calcium and vitamins. Senior dog foods also have ingredients that help your older dog have more energy and a shinier coat.

Besides just choosing which form of food to give your dog, you will need to make sure your dog doesn't have any allergies. There are dog foods out there that are completely grain and gluten free for dogs that cannot tolerate the ingredients. There are also dog foods that do not have artificial ingredients, flavors, or colors. Some dog foods are even tailored to dogs that suffer from diabetes.

HELPFUL TIP
Too Many Choices!

When it comes to purchasing dog food, the choices are abundant! Walking down the dog food aisles can be a daunting experience if you are new to pet ownership. Your breeder and veterinarian are professionals and should be utilized as reliable experts. Doing a search online for "healthiest dog foods" may not be in your dog's best interest, however. Many companies use Search Engine Optimization (SEO) to predict what pet owners will be looking for online. Here is a brief rule of thumb regarding dog foods. Read the labels. If the word "beef" appears on the label, the food should contain at least 70 percent beef. If "beef stew" or "beef dinner" is in the description or name on the packaging, expect that only 10 percent of the product is beef. Be careful when purchasing food if your dog has allergies or special dietary needs. The ingredient list may tell quantity but does not assure the quality of the ingredients in the product.

Choosing the Right Commercial Dog Food

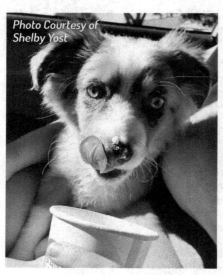

Photo Courtesy of Shelby Yost

As a dog owner, it is your responsibility and choice to choose the correct dog food for your Miniature Australian Shepherd, and educating yourself is the best way to make the right selection and tailor it to your dog's individual needs. In a world where there are thousands of different options, you need to use all available resources to come to the right decision.

Something important to consider when choosing the right commercial dog food is your budget. Some important questions to ask yourself are: Do you have the money to afford some of the brands that are more expensive? Is name brand important to you? Does your dog have to be on a special diet? What brands can your dog's stomach tolerate? Once you sit down and decide what a reasonable budget is, you can make a better-informed decision about the brands of dog foods you are willing to consider.

The internet is a great resource for finding more information about specific brands of food. Search reputable bloggers that raise Miniature Australian Shepherds and see what they recommend. Another way to research dog foods online is to look up online reviews. Serious pet owners will often voice their honest opinions and you can make your own judgment based on the reviews.

You can also ask for recommendations from your veterinarian. After your veterinarian has performed a health check, they will be able to tell you if your pet has any underlying health conditions that need to be considered. They can tell you if your pet is overweight, underweight, has any food allergies, has any diseases, or any skin conditions that need to be taken into consideration.

Based off of their examination of your pet, your veterinarian should be able to recommend the right brand and type of dog food for your Miniature Australian Shepherd. Most veterinary clinics now carry a full range of quality pet foods. This makes it convenient to start your dog on the right foods, right away.

Harmful & Acceptable People Food

At one time or another, humans enjoy giving their pets food that comes from their own plate or diet. This is not a good idea the majority of the time, no matter how much your pet begs! Some of the foods that people wouldn't think are dangerous for dogs are in fact very bad for them. There are foods that can cause health problems or even be fatal to your dog if you are not cautious and keenly aware of what is proper for them.

Foods to Avoid Feeding Your Dog

- **Grapes and raisins**

  Tests have shown that giving dogs grapes or raisins of any variety can cause kidney failure in canines. If your dog ingests them, he could die.

- **Chocolate**

  More than likely you have heard never to give a dog chocolate. The reason behind it is because of the caffeine and the deadly chemicals, theobromine and methylxanthine. These chemicals do not hurt humans, as we digest them quicker than canines, but the toxicity can quickly build up in your dog's system and can cause cardiac failure. Different chocolate varieties contain different levels of toxins.

  Some of the symptoms your dog may exhibit if he has eaten chocolate are vomiting, seizures, tremors, and heart attack. You need to make sure your dog does not have access to chocolate. This is especially true during the holidays when sweets are in abundance.

- **Avocados**

  Avocados contain a deadly poison to dogs which is called persin. Eating avocados (the fruit or the skin) may cause vomiting and diarrhea in dogs. Furthermore, if a dog swallows the pit of an avocado, it can cause bowel obstruction and death unless surgery is performed.

- **Onions**

  Onions contain compounds called disulfides that can damage red blood cells. This causes dogs to develop hemolytic anemia. Dogs can become sleepy, weak, or faint. Onion powder and garlic powder can also have the same effect.

- **Alcohol**

Just as it impairs a human's motor skills, alcohol affects dogs. It can induce vomiting and make your dog very disoriented. Alcohol poisoning is also a very real danger.

- **Salt & Salty Foods**

Letting your pet have access to salt or highly salty foods can be very dangerous. Salt dehydrates the body and if a dog does not have access to enough fresh water, it can cause salt poisoning. Your dog could have stomach issues and seizures if it gets too much salt in its diet.

- **Cooked Meat Bones**

Though we all know our dogs love chicken, pork, and beef bones, giving them to your dog cooked can be hazardous or even fatal. Cooked bones have a tendency to splinter. The splinters can harm your dog's tongue, mouth, throat, or digestive tract. If a dog's digestive tract becomes blocked or ruptured, your pet could need surgery.

Acceptable Human Foods

- **Cooked Meat**

Cooked meat is a great source of protein and minerals for your dog. If properly cooked, you will not have to worry about your dog coming into contact with harmful bacteria such as e. coli or salmonella. Cooked meat is also great for dogs who are off their dog food for health reasons.

- **Baby or Diced Carrots**

Just as in humans, carrots are good for a dog's eyesight. The vitamins

Photo Courtesy of Lisa Cox

and minerals are important to a dog's health. Carrots do not contain many calories, so they can be given to dogs on a diet as a crunchy treat.

- **Apples**

When cut up into appropriate-sized slices, apples are a great treat to give your Miniature Australian Shepherd. Apples contain valuable Vitamin A and

Vitamin C to help boost your dog's immune system. Apples are also known to help clean your dog's teeth!

- **Bread**

  Your dog can have homemade or store-bought bread, as long as he does not have a gluten or wheat allergy. Because bread is high in carbs, it isn't recommended that you feed it to an overweight dog. If you have one that needs to gain a little weight, however, it will not hurt the dog to have it in small amounts.

- **Peanut Butter**

  Raw, unsalted peanut butter is a great treat to give your pooch. Peanut butter is high in protein and moderate in fat. If your dog is a little heavy-set, you may want to be stricter about the amount that you give. Be sure to read the ingredients list to make sure the jar does not contain common artificial sweeteners that are harmful to dogs.

- **Eggs**

  Eggs are a great source of protein for your dog. Eggs can actually be a good item to give your dog if he or she has been vomiting or had loose stools, as they can help settle your dog's stomach.

- **Honey**

  Honey can actually be a great treat for your adult dog in small doses. It contains many of the essential vitamins and minerals that a dog needs. Just as in humans, it has also been known to help dogs with allergies.

Weight Management

"Since Aussies are more active and energetic from other breeds, a high protein diet is a good option. Just be sure not to over feed. An over-weight Aussie can have hip and elbow issues if they are carrying more weight than they should."

Ashley Bryan
Ashley's Aussies

Whether your dog is overweight, underweight, or right where he needs to be, weight management is an important part of being a pet owner. One of the most common and easiest exercises is walking daily. Start out slow and walk the dog around the block the first couple of times. Next, advance your pet to a longer distance by going two blocks. Every few days, you can add more to your walk or you can advance to jogging or running depending on your pet's age and overall health.

Another fun way to exercise your dog is to incorporate play. If a dog enjoys chasing a ball, stick, or Frisbee, give him a daily workout by throwing the object and letting him retrieve it. If your Mini Aussie enjoys the water, you can have him or her go for a swim in a shallow pool, pond, or lake. You can also take your dog to a canine park and let him enjoy the company of other dogs.

Training your dog to do agility courses is also an option to help him lose weight. You can start by buying your pet things such as tunnels to go through, small boards to jump over, and tables to run over. Your pet will learn to exercise and can be entered in contests once it learns the needed commands. The contests will be a way for you and your dog to bond, as effectively training your dog to complete agility courses requires a lot of one-on-one training time.

You can find more information about each of these options in the "Types Of Physical Exercise" section later on.

If your dog is overweight, weight management dog food can be a great addition to steady exercise in order to get your canine companion back to good health. Your vet can recommend the right weight management dog food.

After you choose a dog food brand, it is important that you give it at least a few weeks to work. You can purchase a dog scale for at home or arrange to take your dog back to the vet to check their progress. You need to be observant of any change to his energy levels and if the food is causing any digestive problems. If you see any of these issues it is important that you contact your vet immediately.

You will know that the dog food is working when you see the numbers on the scale starting to go down. Another way is to see if you can feel your dog's ribs better. You may notice that your dog's collar is looser on his neck or that his face looks thinner. Once your pet begins to lose weight he should be much healthier, happier, and full of energy!

Sanitizing Food & Water Bowls

Would you eat out of a bowl that you had eaten lunch from without cleaning it? Probably not. Just as humans prefer clean plates or bowls, dogs appreciate and keep their appetite better if you take the time to properly clean and sanitize their food dishes.

Photo Courtesy of Linda Overbay

There are two basic ways of cleaning dog dishes. The first way is to hand wash your dog's dishes individually. You can wash both the food bowl and the water bowl in the same manner, but remember not to wash your dog's dish with any of your human dishes. The first thing that you will need to do is get a sponge and dish soap. Squirt a generous amount of soap mixed with warm water into the bowl. Scrubbing the dishes with soap will help remove any stuck on food. Wash both the inside and outside of the bowl and then rinse. Most dog food bowls can also be cleaned in a dishwasher if residue is soaked first.

Keeping your dog's dishes clean can help keep your dog healthy. Having a clean bowl helps add an extra level of comfort to your pet's life. It will also help your dog maintain its appetite. All of these things in conjunction help to make your Miniature Australian Shepherd happy!

CHAPTER 8
Grooming Your Mini Aussie

"There is a saying that circulates in the Aussie community: 'Aussies shed twice a year. Each time usually lasts about 6 months.' That being said, Aussies shed a lot! Frequent baths and grooming helps keep it under control."

Cayla Cox
CC Miniature and Toy Australian Shepherds

The Miniature Australian Shepherds' Coat

HELPFUL TIP
Taking Care of Your Dog's Coat

Miniature Australian Shepherds have a double coat; a smooth, short undercoat and a water-resistant, silky outercoat that requires a great deal of maintenance. Mini Aussie owners are encouraged to complete a weekly thorough brushing and detangling to preserve the beauty and health of their dog's coat. Failure to do this may encourage matting. Use a "slicker" brush and dog-raking tool weekly to assist in coat maintenance. NEVER SHAVE your Miniature Australian Shepherd.

Miniature Australian Shepherds have a coat that is much like the standard form of the breed. The hair coat is generally a medium length. The length and thickness of the hair coat can vary from dog to dog.

A Miniature Australian Shepherd's coat goes through a transformation of sorts as it grows and matures. During puppyhood, Mini Aussies tend to be balls of fur and very fluffy. This hair coat usually stays the same until the puppy is around 2 months old, at which point the coat starts its adolescence phase. The coat will generally become much thinner and look more like strands of hair. As the dog matures, the coat slowly gets thicker and turns into its adult form. By two years of age, the adult coat usually grows into its final, fullest stage, although animals may experience individual coat changes again later as they become elderly or after they are altered.

Maintenance is important for all stages of hair growth. The coat must be maintained on a weekly basis to keep the hair coat healthy.

In addition, double coated breeds have summer and winter coats. And the spring and fall changeover between the two seasons brings profuse shedding that can require daily care until the biannual sheds are complete.

Brushes for the Mini Aussie

"Invest in a brush that was designed for double coated dogs. Coat trims are okay during the hot times of the year, but be careful how short it is cut to not mess up the double coat."

Cayla Cox
CC Miniature and Toy Australian Shepherds

Grooming is especially true for indoor dogs if you wish to keep them clean and the furry tumbleweeds to a minimum. In recent years, there have been several innovations in dog brushes to cater to canines with thick double coat layers. Most or all of these brushes should be available at your local pet store or online.

Brand Name	Features/Pros	Cons
Undercoat Rake Brush	• Removes matting from the undercoat and rear of the dog • The metal ends are rounded to keep from scratching your dog's skin • Helps to remove loose and dead hair • Designed to remove stubborn matting from your dog • The other side is to thin and de-shed your dog • Will not scratch your dog	• Better for Mini Aussies with longer coats than for short-haired variants • This comb is not good if your pet has any open sores, as it can aggravate their injuries • Only intended to be used on dry coats
Metal Comb	• Can be used on the entire dog • Gentle on puppies if you have the one with wide set teeth	• Must be used weekly to prevent tangling in the dog's hair
Slicker Brush	• This brush helps to clean dirt and other particles from your dog's fur • Bent wire bristles do not scratch or irritate your dog's skin	• Does not break easily • Not as good for thicker coats
Soft brush	• Soft bristles are easy to train your puppy with before they get an adult coat • Can be used on the face, legs, and feet	• Does not help with mats • Not helpful for brushing thick areas of the coat

Photo Courtesy of
Lindsey Condra
Stillwater Ranch Kennel

Nail Care

Miniature Australian Aussies, like all dogs, can have very sharp nails that require an occasional pedicure. Though they do not mean to do any harm, they can easily wind up scratching your couch or skin. Because of this, it is important to keep nails neatly trimmed.

Education about how to trim nails is readily available online, or you can hire a professional groomer or vet fairly inexpensively to do nails for you. But if you wish to do the task yourself and are worried about clipping the nails too short, there are even nail trimmers that have a built-in sensor to let you know when you're getting too close to the quick of a dog's quick, which will bleed if nicked. You can also choose a low-tech but quality pair of nail clippers if you are confident in your ability to trim your dog's nails at the right length.

The basics of trimming a nail is pretty simple. Knowing where to stop is the trick. To begin, gently grasp your dog's foot and slowly clip off small areas of nail. Pay close attention to where the quick is. The quick is easier to see in white nails than black nails, and looks like a faint horizontal line across the nail. After you clip each nail on a paw, it's a good idea to go back over the ends with the nail file and round the edges until they are no longer sharp or jagged. You will also have to be conscious of the quick when you do this, and you should be careful not to over-file.

Dental Care

Keeping your Mini Aussie's teeth clean is critical to good health. If your dog gets sore gums, a toothache, or an abscessed tooth, bacteria can get into the bloodstream and infect its internal organs.

The first line of defense for your Mini Aussie's dental health is brushing or chews that encourage the dog to scrape plaque off teeth. If you brush, you should brush your dog's teeth every day, or as often as you are able. You will need to purchase a special dog toothbrush as well as dog toothpaste. You cannot use human toothpaste on your dog because the fluoride found in most brands of toothpaste can be poisonous to them. Many dog toothpastes are flavored to help your dog accept them more readily.

Getting a dog to accept teeth brushing is not an easy task. It's best to start when you first get your Miniature Australian Shepherd as a puppy.

Photo Courtesy of Ashley Adkisson

Start slowly and only brush for a short amount of time the first try. Each day that you brush your dog's teeth, slowly increase how long you brush. By the time your dog is an adolescent, he should be used to the process and will accept dental care more easily.

Chews and bones for dental health are usually simple and pretty natural for a dog to take to. Finding something that will clean teeth that your dog will willingly chew is the toughest part. Also, watch that your chew isn't so hard it could break a tooth, and replace it if it becomes a choking hazard, such as when it gets small toward end of use.

You can also buy special plaque and tartar additives for your dog's water bowl. You simply pour a small amount in your dog's water each day. As your dog drinks, the additive will help to reduce tartar, plaque, and other unhealthy buildup that can occur on your dog's teeth. These additives can also help your dog's breath and to whiten their teeth.

Lastly, you should make routine dental checkup appointments with your dog's vet or other qualified professional. This will catch issues when they're small, and help correct any mouth problems before they become worse.

Finding a Professional Groomer

If you don't wish to take on the task of maintaining your pup's hair, nails and teeth alone, establish a relationship with a reputable local groomer. One of the best ways to find a professional groomer is by word of mouth. Don't be afraid to ask other Miniature Aussie owners or your vet for references.

You can also look for groomers online. There are many websites dedicated to rating professional groomers. Seeing the ratings on nearby groomers is as simple as entering your zip code. Read reviews and see what other dog owners think about different groomers before making a choice.

Once you locate the right groomer, make sure they understand what your expectations are. If you want your pet's nails clipped and painted, tell them. If you want your dog to have a certain type of trim, let them know. They can bathe or dip your dog for fleas. They can also do some of the dirty work and clean your dog's anal glands, which helps your dog to not only smell better, but also feel better if they're impacted.

CHAPTER 9
Physical & Mental Health

"If they are loved and feel secure, they are not 'hyper' as many articles suggest, raised right with a sufficient yard to play in they will be content to lay at your feet. Having two is better than one alone if you are at work all day."

Ginny DeLeon
Broken D Bar Ranch

Exercise Requirements For Miniature Australian Shepherds

Miniature Australian Shepherds come from a long line of herding dogs. Herding dogs have the stamina and ability to work extended hours out in the field, in almost all weather, alongside their human companions. As a result of their breeding, Miniature Australian Shepherds require a huge amount of exercise, both mental and physical. It is important that you train them and provide them with brain- and body-stimulating play.

Photo Courtesy of
Devin Neal

Types of Physical Exercise

Physical exercise is something that all dogs need in order to be healthy. Their ancestors were built to travel and to take down prey. They are not naturally sedentary animals. To keep your dog in shape and on track for good physical and mental health, here are some varieties of exercise you may consider.

Walking/ Running: If you live in the city, you can take your dog out for long walks and runs. In cities, it isn't uncommon to see people strolling with their pets down sidewalks, beaches, in parks, or across the street. Because of their active heritage, adult Mini Aussies make ideal partners for racers training for anything from a local fun run to marathons. People who live in less crowded areas are often seen with their Miniature Australian Aussie through a field or down a dirt road. Walking and running are both a form of cardio that is good for your pet's heart, and it encourages bonding between you and your dog.

Just make sure that you stay aware of potential distract in along the route, and you keep a firm grip on your pet's leash. Mini Aussies can be naturally protective of their owners, so remaining confident and focused is important for easing your dog's mind.

Playing Fetch: If you have a large backyard or an available space where you can let your dog run free, you can teach your dog how to retrieve items and bring them back to you. This is a great form of physical exercise for your pooch. You can throw tennis balls, Frisbees, or even a good old-fashioned stick and have your dog run after it. Other items that dogs love to chase are dog toys and rope chews.

Photo Courtesy of
Britt Lastoka

Agility Trials: Some people and their dogs enjoy agility courses. There are classes that will help you learn to train your dog to successfully complete them. Some common obstacles are weaving poles, going through tunnels, jumping over posts, tire jumps, and ladder climbing. Your dog must do all of these quickly and accurately. Because Mini Aussies are historically working dogs, they often love having

Photo Courtesy of Matthew Macesich

a task to complete that will keep them active and earn them love and affection from their owner.

Swimming: Many Miniature Australian Aussies love the water. Finding a shallow place for them to run and frolic is a great form of physical activity. Usually, your Mini Aussie will follow you if you wade out into the water. Swimming is especially great for those pets with arthritis or older dogs that need something a little less strenuous. Some Mini Aussies will even retrieve items from the water if thrown. Just make sure that you don't throw something into the water that is at an unreasonable distance, and that you keep a close eye on your dog at all times.

Playing with Other Dogs: If you have more than one dog, this is an easy form of exercise. You can simply let your dogs out into the back yard and let them play. Dogs are pack animals and do better when they have canine companions. If you do not own two dogs, you can set up play dates with your neighbors or friends dogs or visit nearby dog parks. Just be careful to watch for any aggressive behavior from your dog or other dogs.

Types of Mental Exercise

"Aussies do require an above average amount of exercise. Morning walks and evening walks are ideal. Playing Frisbee is a great alternative to walks and Aussies love the challenge of catching the Frisbee."

Ashley Bryan
Ashley's Aussies

Training with a Clicker

If you are planning on teaching your dog different obedience tricks, you are already on the right path to mentally stimulating him. Dogs have to hear a command and think about what you want them to do. Most dogs can pick up these cues easily. For the stubborn dog, sometimes a clicker is the best answer. The handheld device is used to create a clicking sound that dogs hear and view as a reward. This is because when they do something right, the trainer generally clicks the device and then offers them a treat or food reward. You can find a wealth of information about how to properly use clicker training online or through local training programs.

Scent Work

One way to combat boredom in your Miniature Australian Shepherd is to teach him how to search for items using his nose. You can start with things

HELPFUL TIP
Maintaining Your Dog's Mental Health

Your Mini Aussie is an intelligent, thinking dog that is capable of making decisions. He needs to use his brain and have an extremely active lifestyle to be a happy, healthy pet. The Mini Aussie thrives on routine. Teach your dog to gather his toys and put them in a basket, fetch the newspaper, and pull the clothing basket into the laundry room. Socialize your pet early and often. Introduce the dog to other pets, adults, and children to avoid shyness or aggression with strangers.

Photo Courtesy of Kristen Boyd

that have a distinct smell, such as a favorite treat or toy. Begin by placing the items in fairly easy places to find. In order to guide your dog until he recognizes it as a game, it is best to place him on a lease and issue a command. You can say "find," "search," "go get it," or something similar. Soon your dog will understand that he is supposed to be looking for an object.

Certifications and competitions for scent work is being very popular across North America, so watch for events in your area!

The Shell Game

If you watch TV or movies, you have more than likely seen the shell game. This is where you have three cups, place an object underneath one of the cups, and then mix them up. The person then chooses which cup that they think the object is underneath. You can do this with dogs as well. Due to their incredible sense of smell, they can usually choose the correct cup. You can teach your Mini Aussie to identify the cup with his nose or paw. It makes a fun and interactive game for you both!

Rotate Out Toys

If you purchase new toys every few months, it can be a good idea to change them up with some of the old ones. For example, if you buy your dog a brand new chew toy, put away one or two of their old ones to bring back out at a later time. He will enjoy seeing them again, and it will keep him from getting bored with the same old toy.

Hide-a-Treat Toys

When purchasing toys for your dog, don't overlook the ones that make your dog do some work in order to get a treat! These toys are great for dogs that need a challenge or who are at home alone during the day. It will keep them engaged longer if they are determined to get the treats inside.

Trick Training

Have you ever seen performing dogs on TV? All those dogs know a lot of tricks! Trick training your dog will not only build the bond between the two of you, but will provide structure to your day if you work with your dog for short periods every day. Trick training makes them think about what you are asking of them and makes you work with your dog as a team. There are several different apps and books that can walk you through the steps of each trick to teach it to your dog.

Helping Your Mini Aussie Stay Occupied

Unlike you, your dog cannot watch TV, be on a computer, or a zone into a phone during their free time. Get out and play with your dog every chance you can get. In big cities, there are many options for pet-friendly restaurants, dog parks, and dog salons, and dog support groups have become much more popular this modern-day time.

If you live in a rural area or near parks and trails, just get outside with your dog. Let him follow you around while you work on different projects and stop every now and again to throw a ball or Frisbee. Even if you are simply gardening, your dog will enjoy your company and being able to romp around freely. This is similar to how a Mini Aussie historically spent it's time, when not herding livestock.

Mini Aussies need to have activities that keep them busy and their minds strong, but before picking yours, be sure to research all leash laws for your area.

CHAPTER 10
Routine Veterinary Checkups & Health

Visiting the Veterinary Office

Photo Courtesy of Clair Clauser

Taking your dog to routine veterinary checks is of the utmost importance for your pet's overall health. Puppies need several rounds of vaccines, and later the vet can help you and your dog manage illnesses, parasite problems, weight gain or loss, diseases, reproductive health, and more.

Setting up a veterinary visit is a lot like setting up a doctor's appointment. If you are going to a new veterinarian with a new dog, they will more than likely take your dog's name, ask their age, breed, and get your contact number. All of this information will be put into a file.

Once you get to the veterinary office, the vet or veterinary assistant will get more detailed information. They will ask you for background information that you should have been provided by your breeder. They will want to know if the puppy has had any previous shots or doses of wormer. A good vet will take care not to prescribe your dog unnecessary medication and to make the visit as painless as possible for your canine friend.

The vet will weigh your puppy and do an inspection of their nose, ears, limbs, eyes, and mouth. They will give your puppy any needed vaccinations and record them. They should explain what each of the syringes contains if your pup receives updated vaccinations or shots. They may also do a fecal examination to see if your dog has any worms or parasites. If he does, they will treat the infestation appropriately and most likely schedule a follow-up visit to make sure that the problem has been addressed.

When your appointment is finished, the front desk will schedule your puppy's next visit. Most vets will send you home with a care package after your first visit. The care package may include different dog food brand samples that your vet recommends. It may also have coupons for pet food or toys. Some vets will even give you a doggie toothbrush or a few paper training pads to get started. Usually, it includes vaccination records and a follow-up plan for your puppy to finish the series.

Worms & Other Parasites

Types of Worms

- **Roundworms**
  Roundworms are usually found in puppies, but grown dogs can get them as well. They are typically transmitted when a dog comes into contact with the feces of an infected animal. Roundworms are usually a couple of inches long and look like thin spaghetti noodles. They live inside of your dog's digestive tract and feed off of the food that your dog eats. This can cause your dog to look either emaciated or give him a pot-bellied appearance. If your dog has roundworms, he will often have diarrhea and vomiting as well. He will have to be treated several times in order to eradicate all worms and their larvae.

- **Heartworms**
  Heartworms are caused by a different type of roundworm and are transmitted by mosquito bites. When mosquitoes feed on another animal with worm larvae, they can transfer the larvae to their next victim. Despite the name, heartworms can invade both the lungs and the heart of a dog. Heartworms can cause your dog to develop a cough. The dog will also begin to experience extreme fatigue and become less active. Usually, dogs will begin to lose weight as their heart begins to fail. Symptoms don't usually present in young puppies, because the worms take several months to develop once infected.

Photo Courtesy of Taylor Hall

- **Tapeworms**
  Dogs contract tapeworms by ingesting fleas. Once ingested, the worms attack the dog's intestines. One sign of tapeworms is pieces of the worm in your dog's stool. Another sign could be increased appetite, since the worms are absorbing vital nutrients. Tapeworms are treatable and are not usually harmful to adult dogs. However, they can be fatal in puppies. It is rare for humans to get them from their pets.

- **Hookworms**
  Much like tapeworms, hookworms attach to a dog's intestinal lining. Puppies can contract them in the womb before they are ever born—although you should never experience this if you have chosen a reputable breeder, it is a risk with rescued or adopted puppies. Hookworms can be transmitted through the mother's placenta or even in the mother's milk after the puppies are born. In adult dogs, they can be contracted through fecal matter. These worms can cause anemia, coughing, and skin irritation. Although humans cannot contract them directly, hookworms can become a skin irritation. The larvae can burrow into a person's skin, but will never mature into adults.

Fleas & Ticks

The most irritating pests that you and your dog will have to deal with are fleas and ticks. A tick has eight legs and has a spider-like appearance. A flea looks like a tiny solid black or brown bug. Both are prevalent threats to your dog in the summer, and fleas can remain active in the winter months as well. Fleas and ticks not only make your pet itch, but can also be carriers of dangerous diseases.

As previously mentioned, fleas can carry and transmit tapeworms. If the flea larvae eat a tapeworm egg, it becomes a host. Once the flea gets onto your dog, it causes your dog to itch. Sometimes when dogs itch, they use their mouths to try and remove the flea. If your dog swallows the flea, it will inherit the tapeworm that the flea has been carrying.

Ticks can pass on several diseases, but the two most common are Lyme disease and Rocky Mountain Spotted Fever, which causes small hemorrhages that can damage brain, kidney, liver, heart, and other organs. You will be able to see the small spots appear on areas where your dog does not have fur; they may have a fever or vomit. As soon as you suspect that your dog may be ill, you need to contact your vet immediately.

Lyme disease is another tick-related disease that dogs are very susceptible to. Unlike Rocky Mountain Spotted Fever, a dog infected with Lyme disease may not immediately show symptoms. If symptoms do occur, they typically include inflammation near the bite area, fever, your pet walking stiffly, and problems catching his breath. A veterinarian can provide antibiotics for pets that are infected with the disease.

Choosing to Spay or Neuter

After you adopt your puppy, you will have to make a decision about whether you want to have your dog spayed or neutered. Whether you are interested in breeding your dog, what stipulations were given to you by your chosen breeder, and your dog's gender may all factor into your decision.

One reason to get your Miniature Australian Shepherd spayed or neutered is to limit irresponsible and uneducated breeding. In today's age, it seems like everyone is trying to make money by selling puppies. What people do not realize is that after reputable breeders do all the testing, research, vaccinations, puppy care, etc, they usually do not get rich. Especially when you consider all the time that they spend raising and socializing their litters.

QUOTE
To Chip or Not to Chip?

According to pet-finder.com, the average cost of obtaining a microchip for your dog is $45. Microchips are about the size of a grain of rice and are placed under the skin of your dog by a veterinarian without the need for anesthesia. Microchips are not GPS enabled but are used for radio frequency identification (RFID). When a missing pet is brought to a veterinary hospital or shelter, a wand is passed over the animal to detect if it has been chipped. Each microchip has a unique ID number that the pet owner registers online with a national pet recovery database. Be diligent in keeping your contact information up to date. Any changes in phone numbers or home address need to be kept current on the national database.

Oftentimes, those who adopt dogs lose interest as the dog becomes older or as their life circumstances change to the point that they can no longer accommodate their pup. Some people reading this book won't be able to handle the Miniature Aussie's high energy level. There are also many people who do not have even a basic grasp on the structure, temperament, and genetics of a well-bred dog, then breed their pet quality dog to produce poorly bred and socialized puppies in order to try and make a profit. When this happens, the ill-prepared dogs face negative consequences.

If you are going to breed, then do so responsibly after a deep study into structure, pedigrees, genetic components of personality, and health of the dogs, and after all appropriate testing is completed on your dog. Breeding dogs should meet breed standard. They should be a shining example of the heritage and unique traits the standard is in place to preserve.

Some dogs find themselves in animal shelters. These dogs will be very lucky if a family adopts them. When dogs are not adopted in an adequate amount of time, they are often put to sleep when the shelter reaches capacity and needs space to accept more animals. An exception is no kill shelters and rescues.

If you are considering spaying or neutering, there are many positive aspects to the procedure, but some cons as well. Both are relatively simple procedures. Discuss with your vet and research area ordinances to choose the appropriate time for your pup. Let's discuss what the procedures involve.

Neutering is when a male dog is castrated so it can't reproduce. Neutering doesn't affect the urinary canals of males, nor will it stop them from expressing dominance displays or eliminate behaviors like marking. But it can tone down behaviors that are magnified by sex hormones.

Neutering a male Miniature Australian Shepherd can help with preventing your dog from trying to escape your yard or home, as they will not be searching for females in heat. It also reduces the likelihood of unwanted and poorly bred litters of puppies.

Spaying is the sterilization of a female dog. Spayed dogs will not go into heat if they have a complete hysterectomy. This is helpful because a female dog in heat is not only messy, but can also attract unwanted male dogs to your property, which could impregnate your Miniature Aussie and cause a poorly bred or unwanted litter.

There are 2 commonly used types of spaying. The first is the most common, a total hysterectomy. This is when the veterinarian removes both the uterus and the ovaries. The second is called a tubal ligation which leaves the dog's ovaries intact so she retains the hormones for proper growth and development, but cannot produce any puppies. With this method, the dog can still have a heat cycle unless the uterus is also removed.

After spaying or neutering, make sure your dog has a quiet place to rest and recover per your veterinarian's instructions.

Vaccinations

Vaccinating your Miniature Australian Shepherd is one of the most important aspects of health for your dog. Vaccinations can keep your puppy from getting life-threatening diseases and spreading them to your family or other pets.

Although vaccinations can be costly, they are a critical investment both in the health of your dog and in the health of your family. And they are far less expensive than treating the diseases they prevent!

Common Vaccines

Below are a few common vaccinations given to dogs. Boosters may be recommended at certain intervals by your vet, after the initial dose or series.

- **DHPP:** This vaccine is usually referred to as the "puppy vaccine." It has a combination of different vaccines within one shot. DHPP protects against Lyme disease and hepatitis. Hepatitis can be transferred through blood, saliva, urine, or feces from other dogs or canine species. Canine hepatitis can be contracted through your dog's mouth and nose and can cause kidney and liver disease.
  DHPP also protects against parainfluenza, a respiratory virus that causes dogs to cough and have difficulty breathing. The virus can easily be con-

Photo Courtesy of
Dalton Petru & Bailee Gremmel

tracted from other dogs. Usually, crowded places such as dog parks or kennels that keep a large number of dogs are high-risk areas for your dog to contract a contagious disease. If your dog will frequently be around other pups, this vaccine can be a lifesaver.

Finally, DHPP helps prevent parvovirus. Parvovirus attacks the digestive tracts of puppies. It takes a very small amount of the virus to make your puppy extremely ill. The virus can cause the animal to vomit or have diarrhea. It is generally contracted through the dog's mouth or nose by way of other animals. It is one of the easiest viruses to catch.

- **Kennel Cough:** Bordetella Bronchiseptica, or kennel cough, affects the respiratory system and causes inflammation. It is usually contracted where there are large groups of dogs such as kennels, dog parks, doggy daycares, and other such places. Kennel cough is very treatable, but can be avoided completely through a quick vaccination.

- **Rabies:** Rabies is a fatal disease that affects both the spinal tissue and the brain cells of your dog. Rabies can be transmitted via the saliva of a contaminated animal. Some animals that commonly carry the disease are skunks, coyotes, foxes, bats, raccoons, cats, and opossums. Rabies can take as long as a few months or as little as a week to show symptoms. Dogs will usually become more apprehensive. This apprehension or nervousness will then change to rage. Infected dogs will foam at the mouth and become aggressive, attacking even friends and loved ones, and will have to be put down. There is no known cure, so this vaccination is a must!

It is essential that you make sure your new puppy is up-to-date on its vaccinations. If the breeder that you have purchased from has neglected to do so, you should contact your vet immediately in order to get them caught up.

A suggested vaccination chart from the AKC is listed below:

Age	Recommended Vaccinations	Optional Vaccinations
6 to 8 weeks	Distemper, measles, parainfluenza	Bordetella
10 to 12 weeks	DHPP (vaccines for distemper, hepatitis, parainfluenza, and parvovirus)	Coronavirus, Leptospirosis, Bordetella, Lyme disease
12 to 24 weeks	Rabies	None
14 to 16 weeks	DHPP	Coronavirus, Lyme disease, Leptospirosis
12 to 16 months	Rabies, DHPP	Coronavirus, Leptospirosis, Bordetella, Lyme disease
Every 1 to 2 years	DHPP	Coronavirus, Leptospirosis, Bordetella, Lyme disease
Every 1 to 3 years	Rabies	None

Your pet will need a rabies vaccination booster and a DHPP booster every year.

CHAPTER 11
Socializing with People & Animals

Importance of Good Socialization

"Once your pup has had his shots then you can take him to puppy classes, friend's houses, the pet store, or groomer. Let people into your home and let the pup be held and play with."

Mary Kirkpatrick
Eastcoast Aussies

Dogs are social animals and will thrive when bonding not only with their owner, but with other people and dogs as well. Dogs who are not socialized properly can become unusually aggressive or shy.

Socializing your dog will make them happier and healthier. Not only can it experience reduced anxiety in social situations, such as when you have guests or family over, but also it will be better adjusted to everyday life. A well-socialized dog can travel with you to parks and get along amicably with company.

Ways to Socialize Your Dog with Other Pets

"Start them socializing right away with as many other dogs and puppies as you can. Always try to make it a positive interaction, and ensure that the other dogs are nice dogs to be around. Aussies need a lot of socialization with other dogs. They attach themselves very well to people, but they can be a little standoffish with other dogs if they're not socialized early and often."

Gary Long
Hilltop Aussies

The best time to socialize a dog is when it is a puppy. Puppies can begin the socialization process as soon as their eyes are opened and they are able to use their senses. Though they may be socialized with their littermates and previous owners, you will need to continue the socialization process with them once they are at your home. Here they will experience new people, other animals, and possibly other pets that are already in your home.

When you bring your puppy home, let it get used to the sight, smell, and sound of other people or animals within your home. Start by letting your puppy roam around the areas that he will be able to access. More than likely he will sniff everything and may even try to chew on some things.

You should also expose your puppy to different sounds. Letting him listen to a radio or TV is a good way to help him experience a variety of different

Photo Courtesy of
Nikki Gomez

sounds. You can also acclimate him to the washing machine, power tools, vacuum cleaners, oven timers, and other objects that make loud noises.

An important part of socializing your puppy is addressing habits that are aggressive or antisocial. For example, they may growl at a person while they are eating because they have had siblings that tried to take their food. They may also growl or bite while playing. Finding ways to change these behaviors early on will keep them from cementing and becoming normal as your puppy grows.

Consider balanced training methods. Praise your puppy when they are behaving appropriately and you want to encourage their behavior, but do not be afraid to correct their behavior then reinforce how you want them to behave. If you are having issues with your puppy, start working with a trainer immediately to curb the behavior.

The best way to do this is to consistently be around your puppy. For example, interact with it while it is eating. Be courteous, but let it know you are allowed to pet it, even then.

Discipline your puppy if it growls or nips at you while playing. A simple way to teach your puppy that the behavior is unwelcome is to stop playing and avoid giving him attention for a few minutes. Your new pup will come to understand that this behavior does not lead to the rewards of attention and play. If you neglect to do this, the puppy could show aggression towards other people during these activities.

Properly Greeting New People

"They can get over-excited sometimes and nip at their owners hand out of affection I reach down and tap them on the nose with my two index fingers and tell them: NO"

Gary Long
Hilltop Aussies

It is just as important to teach other people how to approach a dog as it is for your dog to know how to behave when meeting new people. If your dog is meeting someone for the first time and they ask to pet it or approach, you need to make sure to tell them to do so slowly. This gives your dog time to think and to check out the person. It also helps them to see that there is no immediate danger.

Be aware of your dog's habits. If they are nervous in new social situations, make sure to explain that to strangers. Try to remain calm. Your dog will pick

Photo Courtesy of Shari Stevens

up on your anxiety or fear and may become protective or nervous. Meeting and greeting new people should be low-stress and rewarding for your dog.

If your dog struggles around new people, try slowly introducing them to new guests and giving them a small reward whenever they behave properly. Being slow and disciplined is key. It can be difficult to socialize adopted or rescue dogs that have had negative experience with strangers in the past, but all dogs can improve and learn better behaviors through consistent training.

Mini Aussies & Children

A lot of Miniature Australian Shepherds love children. Perhaps it is because they are as active as the dogs themselves. They will lick, jump up to be petted, and even lie down in their laps. Mini Aussies often follow your child around, keep an eye on them, and help them get into mischief.

It is just as important that you train children how to interact with a canine as it is for you to train the dog how to behave. If you get your dog as a puppy, make sure that your children know to be gentle and kind to the dog. Puppies can take some roughhousing, but excess may cause them to become injured. You should also teach your children the appropriate places to touch a dog. For example, many dogs do not want their tails or ears bothered. If a child irritates them, they may be apt to bite.

Children and dogs can be the best of friends. You may find that your Miniature Australian Shepherd even becomes very protective of them. If you teach your child how to behave around your Miniature Australian Shepherd, they should have a relatively harmonious existence together.

HELPFUL TIP
Your Dog's Social Network

Your Miniature Australian Shepherd is, by nature, energetic and intelligent. He will be excellent with children as long as he is kept thoroughly exercised and very busy with jobs and structured playtime. Pent-up energy can quickly turn your happy pet into a badly behaved and destructive dog. Just taking a walk or letting your Mini Aussie out into the yard is not enough to keep this sharp and clever dog mentally and physically at his peak. How much exercise is enough? Your dog needs a schedule of consistent and challenging exercise to mimic the work he's been bred to do. Morning and evening walks are certainly not enough for your Mini Aussie. Schedule ball fetching into your training, "search and rescue" expeditions in the yard or neighborhood, and disk throwing and catching to keep your dog both happy and healthy.

CHAPTER 12
Training Your Miniature Aussie

"Australian Shepherds are incredibly intelligent, and they aim to please. It is important to be patient and kind with training, but more importantly to be consistent with the way you train."

Cayla Cox
CC Miniature and Toy Australian Shepherds

Photo Courtesy of
Ashley Page

Reasons to Train Your Miniature Australian Shepherd

An untrained dog can be a nuisance and a danger. If you want to be a responsible pet owner, then it is vital that you learn either how to train your dog or pay a professional to do it for you.

Photo Courtesy of Kristen Boyd

Mini Aussies are eager to please and incredibly intelligent. Their intelligence only makes it more important that they are trained properly. By giving your new dog clear boundaries, you'll ensure a pleasant relationship for both of you!

Clear Expectations

"Mini Aussies are very, very easy to train. They learn fast and love to please their owners. But they do need to be taught that you are the Alpha over them."

Mary Kirkpatrick
Eastcoast Aussies

You can't expect to train a dog if they don't understand what you want from them. It's important that whether you are giving body signals or oral commands you are very clear and precise on what you want the dog to do. If you are giving hand signals, you cannot be too far away from the dog or they will not be able to clearly see what it is that you want them to do. Likewise, if you mumble a command or say it too softly, the dog may become confused.

Always be sure to use consistent terminology, gestures, and commands. If you want your dog to lie down, pick one phrase and stick with it; likewise, if you choose to use or associate a gesture with the command, do so consistently. Your dog will learn faster and respond better when the expectations set for them are clear.

Photo Courtesy of Kelly More

What Is Operant Conditioning?

When training your dog, using operant conditioning is the best way to produce lasting results. Operant conditioning is simply the presence or removal of a stimulus in response to a behavior—for example, giving your dog a treat for completing a task or scolding your puppy after it goes potty in the house.

Because we cannot communicate with our pets through back-and-forth language, using a clear and consistent pattern of reward and punishment is the most effective way to train a dog. If you stick to the pattern you create, giving positive feedback for desirable behaviors and negative feedback for undesirable ones, your Mini Aussie will quickly learn how to behave in its new home.

Primary Reinforcement

A primary reward is anything that involves the basic needs of your dog. Food, water, shelter, healthcare, or clean conditions are all basic needs that your dog has. These should not ever be withheld during training, though they can be used as supplemental prizes—giving your dog a treat to entice them to perform a certain task, for example.

Kibble, dog biscuits, cuts of meat, or pre-packaged dog treats are all things that a dog both wants and needs. Using food to train helps expedite the process and is a healthy way of training your pooch. When your dog associates being fed with performing a desirable behavior, they will be much more likely to want to perform that behavior.

The same principle applies to rewards such as playtime or toys, as discussed in the section below.

Secondary Rewards

Secondary rewards are the things that your dog wants. For example, your dog will want your praise. Telling him "good dog" after he completes a task and petting him will make him happy and likely to repeat the positive action. Toys are also a good secondary reward option. Dogs can only be allowed to have certain toys after doing what they have been asked to do.

You should never deprive your dog of love or attention in order to preserve it as a reward, but using praise as a mechanism to reinforce good behavior is a great way to encourage your dog to adopt certain behaviors. Mini Aussies are very loyal animals and will want to please their owners! Rewarding them with playtime and a scratch on the head will help them know when they are doing the right thing.

Photo Courtesy of
Matthew Macesich

You can also use clickers to help your dog know when they have performed a good behavior. As your dog associates the sound of the clicker with the outcome of a reward, it will serve as a motivational tool that will help you train them effectively.

Dangers of Negative Reinforcement

ADDITIONAL FACT +i

Perhaps you've chosen a Mini Aussie because you've seen the captivating and beautiful dogs compete in agility competitions or viewed them on television during search and rescue sessions. What you have seen is the result of many hours of dedicated training by both dog and owner. Yes, the Miniature Australian Shepherd has been bred to be a skilled working dog, but this talent does not just emerge; it is fostered and trained.

Spread activities out; a set-in-stone schedule will not provide balance for your dog. Take your Mini Aussie with you while you're doing chores. A trip to the mailbox can be an opportunity to teach a skill. Working in the garden can provide a chance to learn the job of helping clean up tools or gardening debris. Your Mini Aussie will be happiest when he is useful, so take advantage of teachable moments when they arise. When your dog has been successful in his learning, reward him with healthy treats or positive attention. Do not give attention away for free with your Mini Aussie, but always reward desirable behavior generously.

While positive corrections help to reinforce good behavior, negative corrections can have the effect of causing a dog to be shy, scared, or aggressive toward you. Associating good behavior with good outcomes is generally a safer and more effective way to train your dog than by associating bad behavior with bad outcomes.

Providing your dog with rewards for performing the appropriate behavior will cause your dog to understand that if he does not listen, he will not get the things that he wants. Positive correction can include firmly telling your dog no and giving it a reasonable punishment. However, you should never strike your dog in any way, ever.

This can lead to your dog being afraid of you and the point of training is not that the dog obeys out of fear, but out of obedience. Enforcing negative correction can also lead to a dog becoming aggressive and attacking you in order to protect itself.

Another form of negative correction is denying the dog basic needs such as those discussed above. These are things a dog can't live without and should never be withheld. A child may learn from you taking away a toy, but a dog cannot comprehend why you are doing it. Instead of it being a punishment, it could backfire. For example, if you take away your dog's favorite chew toy, it could result in the dog tearing up your brand-new pair of shoes, because it has nothing else to chew on. This would only lead to the dog being further in trouble.

Similarly, never punish your dog for behaviors that were performed hours before. Dogs often have trouble understanding why they are being punished if the associated behavior is not immediate or recent. Delayed punishment could cause your dog to become more confused, anxious, or afraid.

Professional Training

If you are struggling to train your dog, it may be time to bring in a professional. Always find a reputable trainer, either by looking at reviews online or by speaking with friends or community members who have had to use a dog training service. A quality dog trainer will be gentle but firm in explaining how you can help your dog learn.

Alternatively, you can attend classes with your dog. These group sessions will give your dog the opportunity to learn and socialize simultaneously, and the trainer leading the class can give you feedback on how to effectively train your dog.

However you choose to train your Mini Aussie, remember that your dog—especially as a puppy—will make mistakes. There will be times when you are upset or frustrated with your dog. That is normal. Each dog learns differently, and training your dog effectively requires dedication. Don't give up!

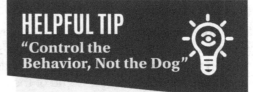

HELPFUL TIP
"Control the Behavior, Not the Dog"

It is important to be consistent while training your Mini Aussie. Purposeful training for commands like sit, stay, come, and drop are essential to a well-behaved dog. While teaching a new command, follow up with positive reinforcement preferably healthy small bits of food or treats. Feeding treats when not linked to training activities is not recommended. While training should and can be completed at any time during the day, it makes sense to coach the dog when he hasn't just finished eating. He will be more responsive and attentive if he does not have a full tummy. Remember that a firm, kind, and consistent approach is best when training any animal.

CHAPTER 13
Commands

"People read how smart they are but they really don't have a clue until they have actually raised one. Extremely smart!!!"

Cindy Harris
Rocky Top Kennels

What commands you decide to teach your dog will depend on whether or not you want to enter your dog in competitions, how frequently your dog will be around guests or strangers, and how much you as an individual enjoy training your dog.

However, it is important that you follow the procedures outlined in the previous chapter if you want your dog to learn well and quickly. Choosing the right rewards for your dog and maintaining consistency are key.

When training your dog with any command, make sure you keep the lesson fairly short. This means no more than 5-10 minutes at a time, and always end on a good note! Remember, Rome wasn't built in a day, and neither was an obedient dog! Below are some of the most common commands that dog owners use to help their canine companions be more obedient and respectful.

Photo Courtesy of
Shelby Yost

Basic Commands

Sit

To train your puppy to sit, gently push down on his bottom. Their first instinct will be to pop back up. Some puppies will think it is a game, so you will have to be persistent. Keep pushing their bottoms down until they stay in the sitting position.

Alternatively, you can hold a treat just in front of your puppy's nose and slowly lift it. As you move the treat, he will instinctively move toward a sitting position. As soon as he sits, offer praise, your predetermined reward, or use your clicker.

Lie Down

Once you have taught your dog to sit, you have laid the foundation of teaching him to lie down. Give your dog the "sit" command. When he sits, move a treat toward his nose so he follows it. Slowly drop your hand down toward the ground. The dog should once again follow your hand. Bringing his front end down will place him in the "lie down" position. If he correctly

105

follows this sequence, reward him with the treat and offer praise, reinforcing the verbal command— "Good boy! Lie down!"—however, if he tries to stand up and follow the treat, gently retract your hand and tell him to sit.

It is important to only offer your dog the reward if they successfully complete the action, and to reiterate the verbal command in a positive way each time they succeed.

Stay

Photo Courtesy of Sara Hazen

Training your dog to stay can be very difficult. Most dogs will want to follow you, especially if you're holding a treat. If you have done the pre-work of teaching them to sit and lie down, you have a good start. The first thing you should do is to get your dog to either sit or lie down.

After he does what you have asked, slowly back away, still facing him. Most people add a hand signal or gesture, such as holding out a hand in the universal gesture for "stop." If you have done the groundwork with sit and lie down, your dog should stay put for at least a few moments.

If he does as he is told, you may then call him and offer a treat. Once your dog starts to follow the command, try going further away from them each time. This will help him know that stay means stay. Once your dog starts to learn that he should not follow you when you back away, try leaving your dog's sightline for a few moments at a time.

Come

Another one of the basic commands your dog will need to know is "come." It should be taught in conjunction with "stay." As with other commands, it is important to choose a consistent command before you begin training—with the "come" command especially, dog owners have a tendency to use a variety of language, but your pup will respond better if you choose a single phrase and stick to it.

Photo Courtesy of Amanda Akagi

Start by making your dog sit or lie down. Then tell him to stay. Walk a ways away and then face him. Pat your leg or whistle before you give the command so that he knows what you want him to do. The dog should get up from the stay position and come directly to you. If he does not, use a treat to lure him over to you and use your chosen command to associate the action with your command.

Most dogs pick up on this command easily, but it is absolutely crucial that your dog understands how important it is to come when called. If your dog gets out of the yard, is approached by an aggressive dog or animal, or if your dog is in a dangerous situation such as being out in the middle of the street, it is imperative that your dog comes when called.

Drop It

Miniature Australian Shepherds love a game of fetch. Teaching them to fetch with their favorite toy is highly recommended. To teach drop it, they will need to have the "come" command mastered.

Start by tossing the dog's toy away so he chases it. As soon as he reaches it and picks it up, give the "come" command. Because most dogs won't want to let go of the toy, they should return with it. When the dog reaches you his instinct will be to pull away if you grab the toy. You need to very firmly tell the dog to "drop it."

Most Miniature Aussies are not aggressive and are very loyal toward their owner, so you

HELPFUL TIP
Dealing in Dog Currency

Dogs value shelter, water, food, and attention. Train your Mini Aussie by exchanging what he values with your goals for him. Use small treats of food, perhaps even kibble, during repetitive training sessions. Keep the treats small and easy to chew during these lessons. Use higher-valued rewards during difficult training that requires your dog's full and undivided attention. Rewards such as liver bites are prized treats for a difficult task well done. Be mindful of the value of the reward you're offering your dog. Using highly prized treats for easier behavior modification can change the value of the reward. Balance is the key when training your Mini Aussie.

*Photo Courtesy of
Lindsey Condra
Stillwater Ranch Kennel*

most likely will not have to worry about the dog being aggressive toward you—however, you should always exercise caution when first teaching a dog this command, as some dogs can be very possessive about toys, food, and other property.

The first few times the dog will want to play tug of war with you in order to keep the toy. Once he releases the toy, give positive reinforcement, before throwing the toy again. After this is repeated many times, he will pick up that "drop it" means releasing an item from his mouth. This command can also be useful if your dog ever picks up something dangerous—the last thing you want to do if your pup has something nasty, sharp, or contaminated in its mouth is chase him down!

Roll Over

To teach your dog to roll over, you will need treats. Make sure you have the dog in the lie down position. You will use the treats to lure the dog into doing what you want. Lure the dog so that it is lying on its side.

After your dog learns to lie on its side, move the food further above its head. This should make the dog flip over or roll. The dog will learn to roll all the way over to get the reward.

Off or Down

Ideally, you have taught your Mini Aussie not to jump on strangers—however, if your dog is excited or in an unfamiliar location, knowing the "off" or "down" command can help you to quickly establish rules in new locations. It can also help to keep your dog safe if he is trying to jump onto or climb something dangerous.

Advanced Commands

Speak or Bark

Enticing your dog to speak is a bit more difficult than teaching basic commands. To teach your dog this trick you will need treats. Dogs do not bark just to bark. They bark when they become very excited or something piques their interest.

You can either run and let your dog chase you, get a favorite toy and play keep away, or roughhouse with your pup in order to get him wound up. Once he begins to bark, show him a treat. When he does bark, praise

Photo Courtesy of
Jennifer Wagner
Eldorado Ranch Mini Aussies

Photo Courtesy of Natasha Wice

and reward him with a treat. This command can take a lot of time for some dogs to pick up, so be patient.

Heel

The "heel" command is taught when you want your dog to walk right by your side. This can be a command that is used with or without a leash. To teach it, however, you need to have a leash on the dog. To start, place the leash on the dog and step right beside him. Tug on the leash and walk as he walks. If the dog falls out of step, whether staying in front of you or behind you, stop abruptly and do not allow him to go further. If your dog does as you ask and walks beside you, give him a treat. Eventually he will get the idea of what this command means.

This command is particularly important if you live in a crowded area where there are a lot of distractions. In order to keep your dog safe, you want them right by your side—when your dog wanders away from you, they could approach another dog or venture into the street.

Spin

You can teach your dog to spin in a circle with a treat and a hand motion. Show your dog a treat and hold it up to make sure that he is paying attention to it. Once he is standing in front of you and watching, take the treat and place it about a foot away from his nose. Keeping your hand elevated, slowly move the treat in a circle or spinning motion while giving the command. If your dog is paying attention, he should follow the treat and turn around. When the dog does as asked, give him the treat. Repetition will help you and your pet to perfect this trick.

Shake or Paw

In order to learn this trick, your dog will need to already be trained to sit. After giving the sit command, gently reach down and pick up your dog's paw. Making sure you use the same paw each time, say "paw" or "shake" while doing this. When the dog has done as you have asked, give him a treat. Keep practicing until your dog lifts his paw when you give the command.

CHAPTER 14
Giving Your Miniature Australian Shepherd a Job

"Aussies are herding dogs, they need something to do otherwise they may pickup bad habits like herding the kids around the house. Stimulate their minds by throwing a ball or taking them for walks. A bored Aussie is one that will get into mischief."

Robert Kidd
Kidd's Toy Aussies

Herding dogs

HELPFUL TIP
"Help Wanted"

What are your goals for your Miniature Australian Shepherd? Have you added your new dog to your family for a particular purpose? Whether you want your Mini Aussie to herd, become a service or therapy dog, or for enjoyment, careful and patient training is key to success. Your dog has been bred to be an active worker, but it is up to you to know your goals and train for achievement of those goals.

The original Australian Shepherd from which the Miniature Australian Shepherd was derived was bred for use in herding cattle and sheep. Although minis are popular in settings off the farm today, it is not uncommon to still see them performing these same historic functions today. They are seen frequently among equine enthusiasts hitting the road, as well as farmers and ranchers who prefer slightly more compact helper.

If you purchase a Mini Aussie and own livestock, consider training your dog to herd. Miniature Australian Shepherds can be especially useful if your sheep or other livestock are not docile and need to be moved to a new area. If you want your dog to be able to work the animals and not just be chasing, you will need to consult with someone who is an expert in training herding dogs. This can make your life much easier and potentially keep your dog out of trouble by teaching it that it shouldn't just run after animals for sport.

Therapy Dogs

Even though Miniature Aussies are known for their rambunctious nature, they become calmer as they mature, and this milder demeanor makes many an ideal choice for hospital therapy dogs. Aussies have an innate loving nature, and are kind and loyal.

Therapy dogs are generally found in health care facilities or schools. These may range from hospitals, physical therapy or occupational therapy clinics, nursing homes, schools with occupational therapy services, schools with physical therapy services, or other places where patients are cared for.

Therapy dogs should not be confused with service dogs. Their main purpose is to visit a facility and to provide comfort and affection to the patrons. If a patient is stuck in a hospital bed, the therapy dog may be brought to them so that they can interact with the dog. Therapy dogs do not do any actual tasks for the patients other than being companions for a short visit.

ADDITIONAL FACT

If your intention is to utilize your Miniature Australian Shepherd as a therapy dog, be certain that your dog's training is focused toward this goal. Therapy Dogs International (TDI) is an excellent place to start. Their website, tdi-dog.org, gives an overview and specifics about the requirements for dogs/handlers who want recognition and registration to use their dog as a therapy animal. Age and health requirements of the dog, as well as the character of the handler, are prerequisites to being tested. The evaluation starts when the dog and handler are first observed by the TDI Certified Evaluator. From time to time, a person with a disability may have the need for both a service dog and therapy animal. TDI does not certify service dogs but may evaluate two separate dogs concurrently. If you plan on using your Mini Aussie for visits to local hospitals, nursing facilities, or for other public uses, you should check the rules and regulations of each facility before entering with your animal. Please note that TDI requires insurance for their registered dogs and handlers. Know the facts before attempting to use your Mini Aussie as a therapy dog.

Therapy dogs can really help boost the morale of a child or adult who is struggling. They can also help to soothe geriatric patients in nursing homes who are ill, lonely, or reaching the ends of their lives. The comfort they provide is very valuable.

If you are interested in pursuing a certification for your dog, you can do so through the American Kennel Club or a third-party program. Your dog will, at minimum, need to know commands related to personal safety such as sit, stay, down, heel, and come.

Photo Courtesy of
Taylor Hall

Service Dogs

Service dogs are canines that are used to help people with disabilities in their everyday lives. For instance, a person who is blind may have a Seeing Eye Dog to guide them or a person who has uncontrollable diabetes might have a diabetic alert dog who senses when their blood sugar is becoming abnormal. Some Mini Aussies may be too sensitive to their owners and have a tendency to feed off of what their owner is feeling, to be ideal for this type of work. However, others find the right balance to be wonderful.

Photo Courtesy of
Ashley Himmelsbaugh

Under the American Disabilities Act (ADA), service dogs are the only kind of dog who has public access rights. Public access rights mean that the dog can go everywhere with their owner who has a disability.

Those who claim to have a dog certified as a service dog from an online website are mistaken, since service dogs are not certified by any company. Service dogs, according to the ADA, help mitigate a disability for their handler. If their handler does not have a disability that the dog is trained to mitigate so that they can function more normally, then it is not a service dog.

Emotional Support Dogs

Let's discuss emotional support dogs. These are very different than service dogs by definition. Emotional support dogs do not have public access rights, which means that they are only allowed in pet friendly places. People with anxiety, depression, or other mental health disorders can benefit from these types of dogs. The dogs are a source of comfort and can help some-

Photo Courtesy of Suzanne Transier

one having an anxiety attack or in the midst of a depressive episode to feel calmer and less alone.

Emotional support dogs do not require special training, but their owners must have a note from a psychiatrist, psychologist, or therapist in order to verify that they are indeed an emotional support dog.

Entertainment Dogs

Miniature Australian Shepherds were first used as entertainment dogs at rodeos in addition to their livestock herding job. They are natural born performers and love attention! Because of this, they are an easy choice for anyone who wants a very athletic dog to perform tasks or tricks.

Miniature Australian Shepherds have a great jumping ability. They are able to jump through hoops, grab Frisbees out of the air, and complete agility courses. They are great candidates for all kinds of canine athletic competitions!

Miniature Australian Shepherds are incredibly smart and respond to commands well. This capability makes them a good choice for dogs that can be used in movies, commercials, and even plays. The Aussie's ability to learn and want to please can make them a ready choice for filmmakers who need dogs who can stay for long periods of time, play dead, or recreate rescue scenes.

Other Jobs

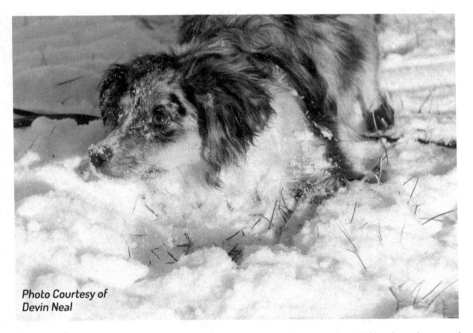

Photo Courtesy of
Devin Neal

At the end of the day, working dogs like Australian Shepherds—and subsequently Mini Aussies—are happier when they are able to fulfill a purpose, but that doesn't mean that you have to bring your dog to hospitals or to homes for the elderly. Mini Aussies thrive when they are challenged, loved, and valued. They enjoy working and having a job, no matter how it showcases their strengths.

Simply by dedicated one-on-one time to training your dog, playing with them, and engaging them, you will help your dog live a happier and healthier life. Because Mini Aussies are so smart, they will quickly pick up on any new task you give to them—think of ways to challenge your Mini Aussie and keep them learning. They will love it and so will you!

CHAPTER 15
Advanced Mini Aussie Health & Aging Care

It is a strange thing, watching your dog grow old. After so many years of shared memories, it can be difficult and saddening to see your dog experience the traumas of old age and become less spry. Mini Aussies usually live to anywhere from 13-15 years old, and their care should be treated accordingly as they get older.

Certain diseases are common in older dogs. Although these are not necessarily breed specific, it is good to be aware of them so that you can be prepared to address these as your dog ages. However, if you purchased your dog from a reputable breeder and have access to information regarding your dog's genetic lineage, you may be able to get an understanding of what specific threats your dog may face as it ages. Or what quality breeding choices made before the dog even existed safeguarded it from!

Photo Courtesy of
Kristen Boyd

Common Aging Diseases

Hip and Elbow Dysplasia: Hip dysplasia involves very painful arthritis in a dog's hip area. It can affect a dog's comfort and walking, eventually causing a permanent limp. Hip dysplasia occurs when the hipbone no longer fits into the pelvis' socket. this is usually caused by the wear and tear of bone and cartilage. The amount of pain that a dog with the condition feels varies for each individual. Elbow dysplasia works much in the same way as hip dysplasia. The only real difference is that it affects the front legs of the dog instead of the rear. The dog's front joint or elbow can become dislocated or worn down and cause the dog mobility and pain issues.

Cancer: Older dogs have a relatively high rate of cancer-related deaths. Most cases of cancer are diagnosed when a dog is in its later years of life. Most dogs will suffer from either lymphoma, which attacks the immune system, or hemangiosarcoma, a tumor or tumors that can form anywhere that there are blood vessels within the dog. If you suspect your dog may be suffering from cancer, it is always best to take it to your family vet. It is relatively common for dogs to develop benign tumors in their old age, which may be unsightly but are not a threat to your dog's wellbeing.

Cataracts: Although Miniature Australian Shepherds of any age may get them, cataracts are more prevalent during a dog's older years in life. Cataracts in the dog's eyes can eventually render them blind. If a dog gets one in one eye, it will inevitably get one in the other. A blind dog will take lots of extra care, especially if that dog is an elder.

Photo Courtesy of
Sheri Baldwin

Illness & Injury Prevention

"Australian Shepherds are prone to MDR1 -multi drug resistance gene. You MUST get your puppy tested for MDR1. A puppy with MDR1 can have a fatal reaction to certain medications that are common in routine spay/neuter procedures, dental cleanings and even flea/tick medications. Testing your puppy only costs $60 and it is a simple cheek swab that you mail to a testing clinic. More information can be found at: http:// vcpl.vetmed.wsu.edu regarding MDR1."

Ashley Bryan
Ashley's Aussies

As your dog becomes older, you will need to help your pet be more careful to prevent unnecessary injury. As dogs age, their bones, joints, and teeth become more brittle. Though dogs generally slow down, they may still be reckless or "act like a puppy." There are also products like pet stair steps to help older animals traverse multistory houses.

You need to make sure to monitor the health of your dog's teeth by brushing them, providing dental chews, and regularly getting vet checkups. Dogs often wear their teeth down over the years and will need softer foods and smaller kibble in order to avoid damaging or breaking their teeth.

If your dog is an outside dog, you will need to take into consideration his age before leaving him outside in the summer or winter. Young dogs can tolerate the heat or cold better. Their blood circulation and fat content is usually higher than that of an older dog. Older dogs can also have weather-related arthritis that flares up during the chillier months. No dog should be left outside during intense weather events, but consider bringing an older dog in earlier and during milder weather, as they lack the resources they once had to cope with the elements.

`It is recommended that, as your dog ages, you increase the frequency of visits to the veterinary office. It is not unusual for an aging dog to go see a veterinarian every six months for a health checkup. Your vet will be able to perform tests and keep you informed on how you should be adjusting diets and daily routines. They can monitor heart activity and check for any underlying problems.

Senior Dog Nutrition & Exercise

HELPFUL TIP

As you watch your Mini Aussie age, you will notice changes in health, diet, and sleep patterns. Perhaps more frequent trips to the vet may be required as your dog ages. Consult your veterinarian about dietary adaptations and adjustment of exercise for your senior pet. A dog's best friend is his owner, and the time may come when you must make some heartbreaking decisions. Always be cognizant of quality of life for your companion. With care, training, and affection, your Miniature Australian Shepherd will be a loyal, trusted friend and family member for many years.

As your dog comes into the later stages of its life, its nutritional and exercise needs will greatly differ from when it was a puppy and growing adult. Older dogs generally do not require the same large amount of calories each day that a younger dog does. Changing your dog food to one lower in calories can help to prevent your Miniature Australian Shepherd from becoming too obese.

Older dogs are not as active and have weaker metabolisms as compared to their younger counterparts. They do not burn calories as efficiently and will need food with a balanced level of nutrients in order to maintain a healthy weight.

Luckily, there are now many varieties of senior dog foods available for purchase. Not only do these foods have the correct amount of calories and minerals, but they can also appeal to a variety of disorders that an older pet may incur. For example, there are special foods for dogs with diabetes, allergies, or dogs with fiber disorders. It is highly recommended that you talk to your vet or do research before selecting a dog food for your aging Mini Aussie.

You will find that older dogs often need just as much exercise as younger dogs. The difference is the intensity and frequency of the exercise. You do not want to push an older dog to run or walk as quickly as a younger dog would. If you play fetch, try not to throw the ball or toy as far away as you would have in the dog's younger days.

Break up exercise into several short walks per day. If your pet has joint problems, swimming is a low-impact exercise that will help your dog exercise without putting undue strain on their joints. If you do not have a nearby body of water, or if you cannot afford to bring your dog to a physical therapist with access to a pool, you can invest in a small portable pool online that you can fill straight from a hose.

Common Old Age Ailments

As your Mini Aussie gets older, there will be days where he just does not feel well. Some of the common ailments or problems that you may notice are:

Stomach Issues: Older dogs' stomachs may not always process food as easily as they did before. Dogs can get such things as heartburn and indigestion. This can in turn, cause them to either vomit or have diarrhea. If an upset stomach occurs, it will generally pass within 24 hours. If it does not, it might be a good idea to contact your vet.

Fatigue: Older dogs will require more sleep. In fact, you shouldn't be surprised if he sleeps for more than half of the day. You may notice that after your daily walks, your dog is eager to find its favorite dog bed or quiet place and drift off to sleep. This is because older dogs tire much faster and need to conserve energy. You should allow your dog to sleep and shouldn't become too concerned unless other problems are present.

Bladder Issues: An elderly dog will need to relieve its bladder more frequently. Just as when he was a puppy, it will be harder for him to hold his water for long periods of time. If he is an inside dog and you will be gone for a long period of time, you need to make sure and have a puppy pad available or a doggy door that is easily accessible. Don't be surprised at accidents, even though your dog has been potty trained for years. Older dogs can become incontinent and leak—they do not do it on purpose, so don't punish them.

Eyesight and Hearing: Old dogs may eventually begin to lose both their eyesight and hearing. This can be very difficult for you as an owner as well as for the dog itself. Changes will have to be made in order to accommodate your dog. When a dog becomes blind or hard of seeing, it will generally become less mobile. You will need to rearrange items such as its food, water bowl, and bed so that they are more easily accessible and simple for your dog to find. You will also have to be more diligent about taking your dog outside to relieve itself.

If a dog loses its hearing, it will no longer be able to hear you to follow your commands. It will also not be able to hear sounds that can signal danger. Always be extremely careful when talking your dog outside once it has lost some or all of its sight or hearing—your Mini Aussie may put himself in danger without knowing it.

Photo Courtesy of Kelly More

Saying Goodbye to Your Pet

Sooner or later, there will come a time when you will have to tell your beloved Miniature Australian Shepherd goodbye. Whether it's from old age, injury, or a medical condition, it isn't an easy decision to make. When deciding whether it's time to say goodbye, consider the following:

- Is your dog suffering?
- Can your vet no longer give him anything to ease the pain?
- Is the dog likely to get any better?
- What is his current quality of life?
- Is it cost effective to prolong the inevitable?

There are no easy decisions about choosing whether or not to put your dog down. If your Mini Aussie is suffering or is in excessive pain, it may be the right decision to say goodbye. It will always be a hard decision, but sometimes it's the right one. Give your pup their favorite meal, take them for a long walk (if they are able), and give them plenty of love—they have had a good life, and they deserve to say goodbye peacefully.

Your vet will be happy to give you a moment alone with your dog so that you can say goodbye. You can be in the room or not, but your Mini Aussie will always be with you either way.

CONCLUSION

Mini Australian Shepherds are excellent friends, loyal companions, and intelligent partners in crime. Making the decision to adopt, buy or rescue a Mini Aussie should not come lightly. The breed is energetic, quirky, and full of surprises; but at the end of the day, your Mini Aussie will be your best friend.

If you take good care of your Mini Aussie, he or she will take good care of you. Life will be different with your new furry friend—but it will also be much, much better!

Photo Courtesy of
Haley Sullivan

CPSIA information can be obtained
at www.ICGtesting.com
Printed in the USA
BVHW091203181022
649722BV00004B/44